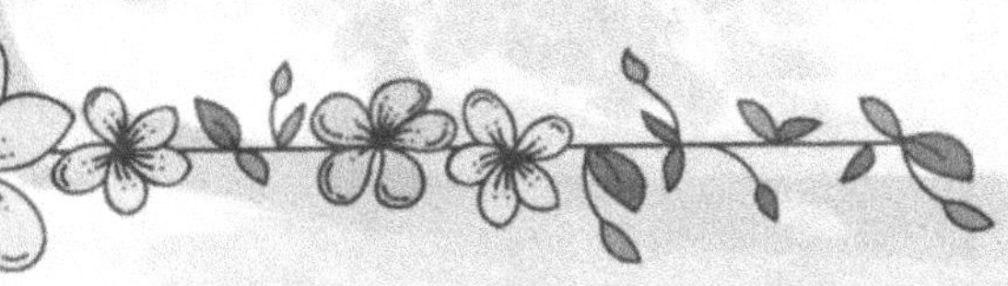

"The bamboo
that bends is
stronger than
the oak that
resists."

Japanese Proverb

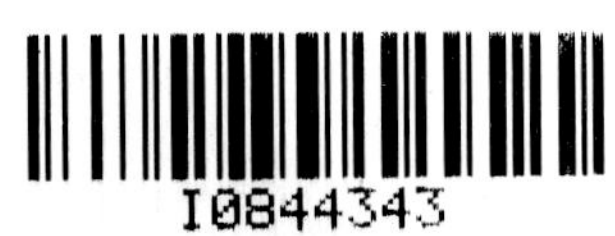

My painting book

Name--------------------------------

Date --------------------------------

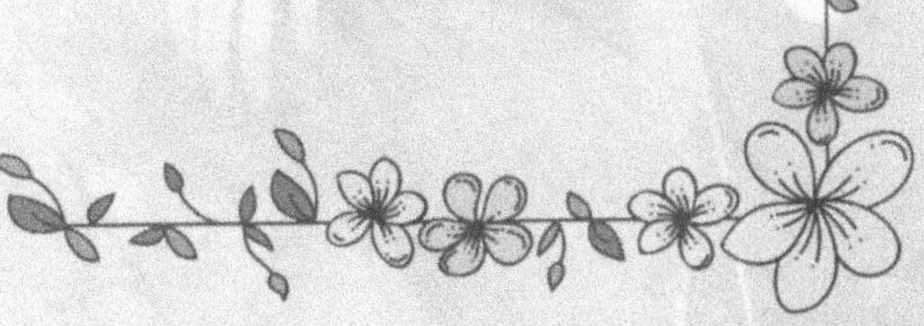

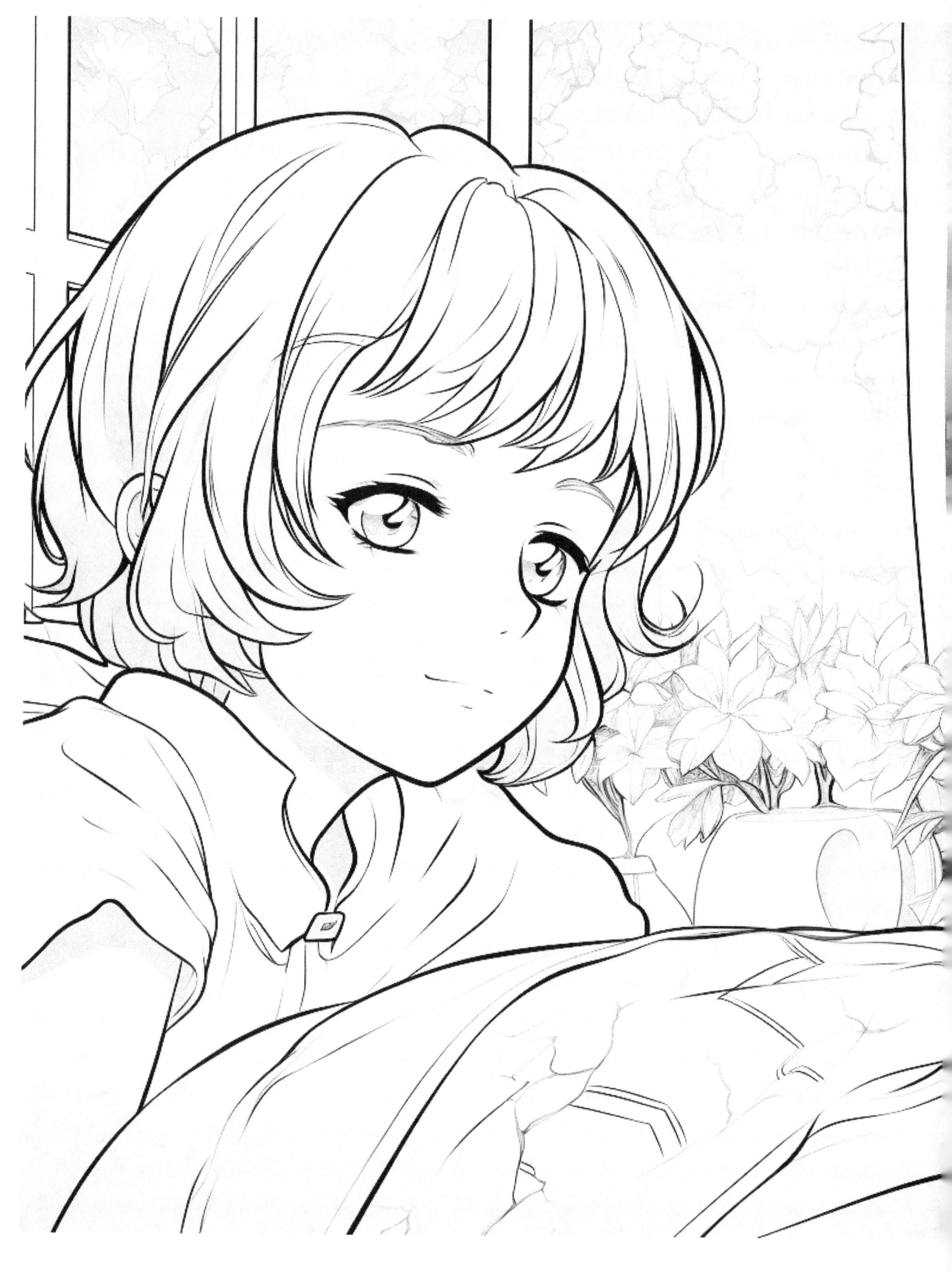

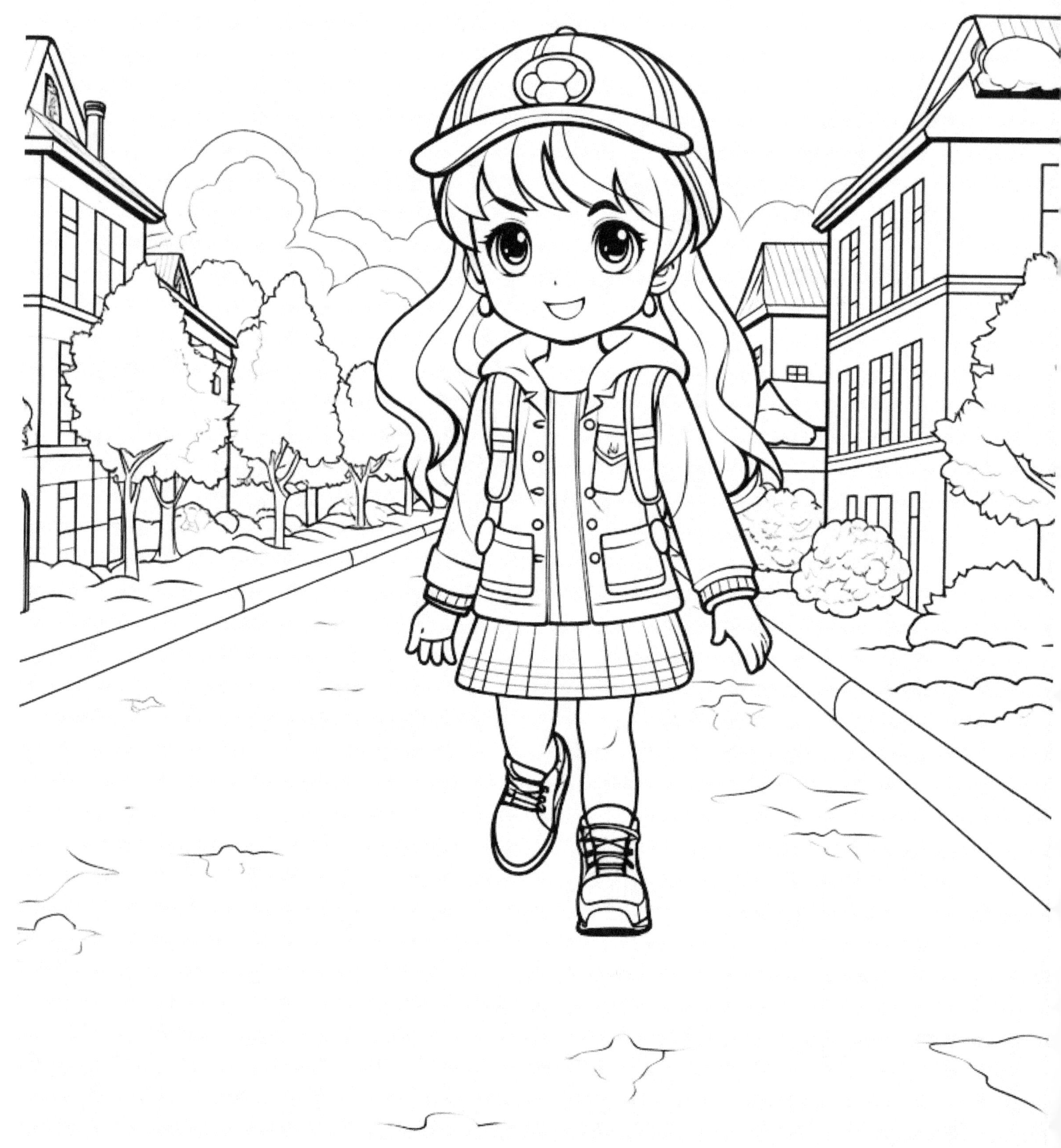

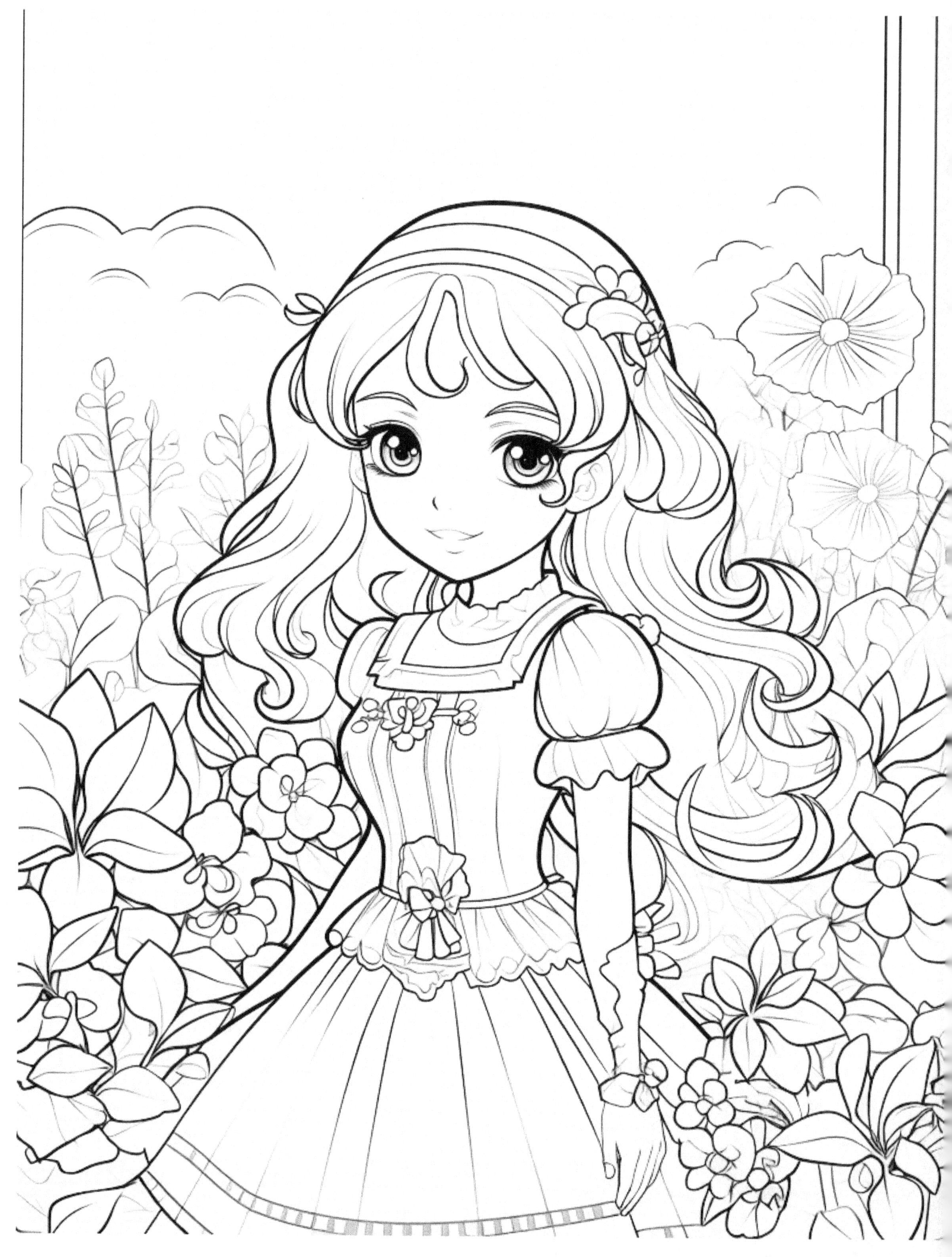

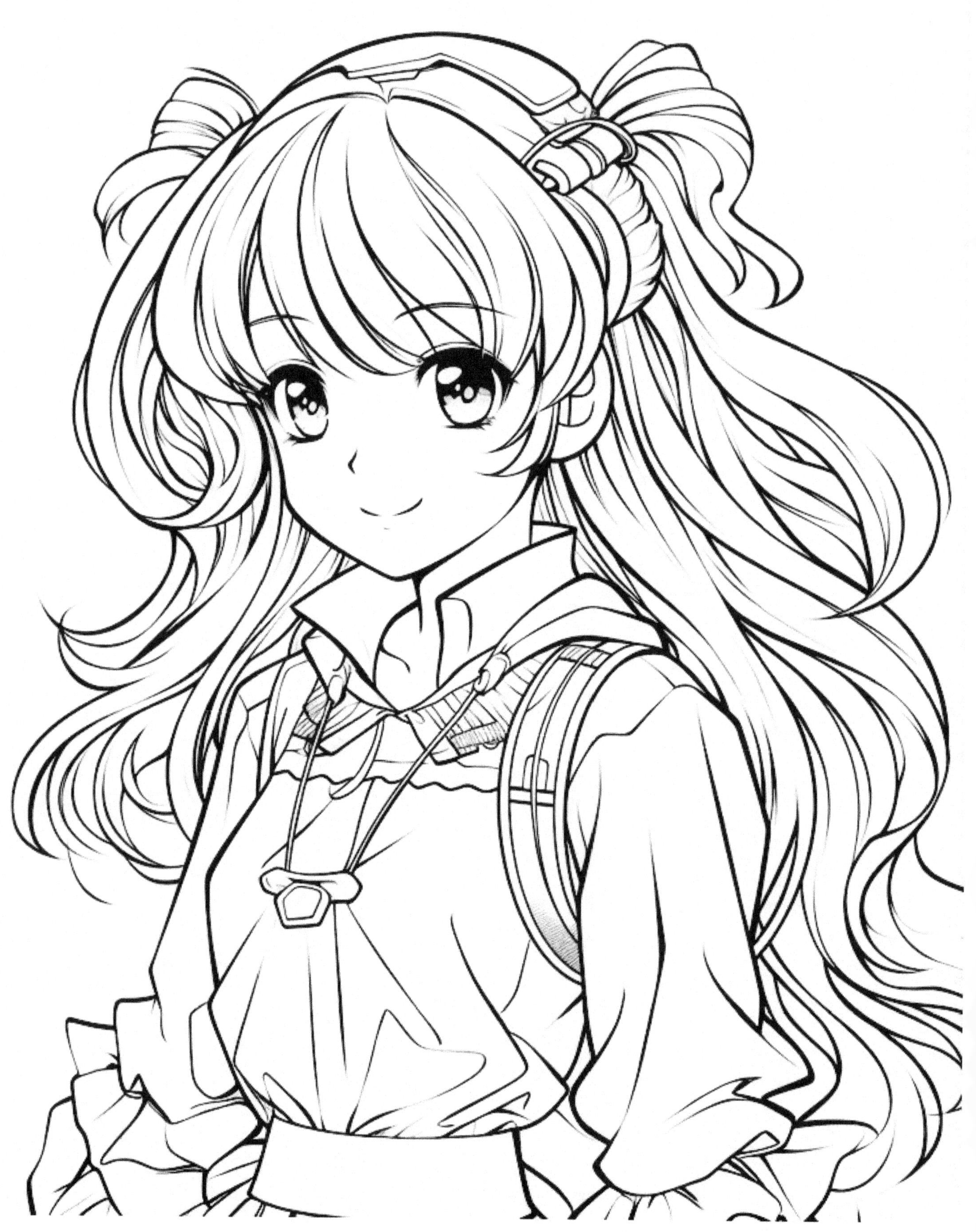

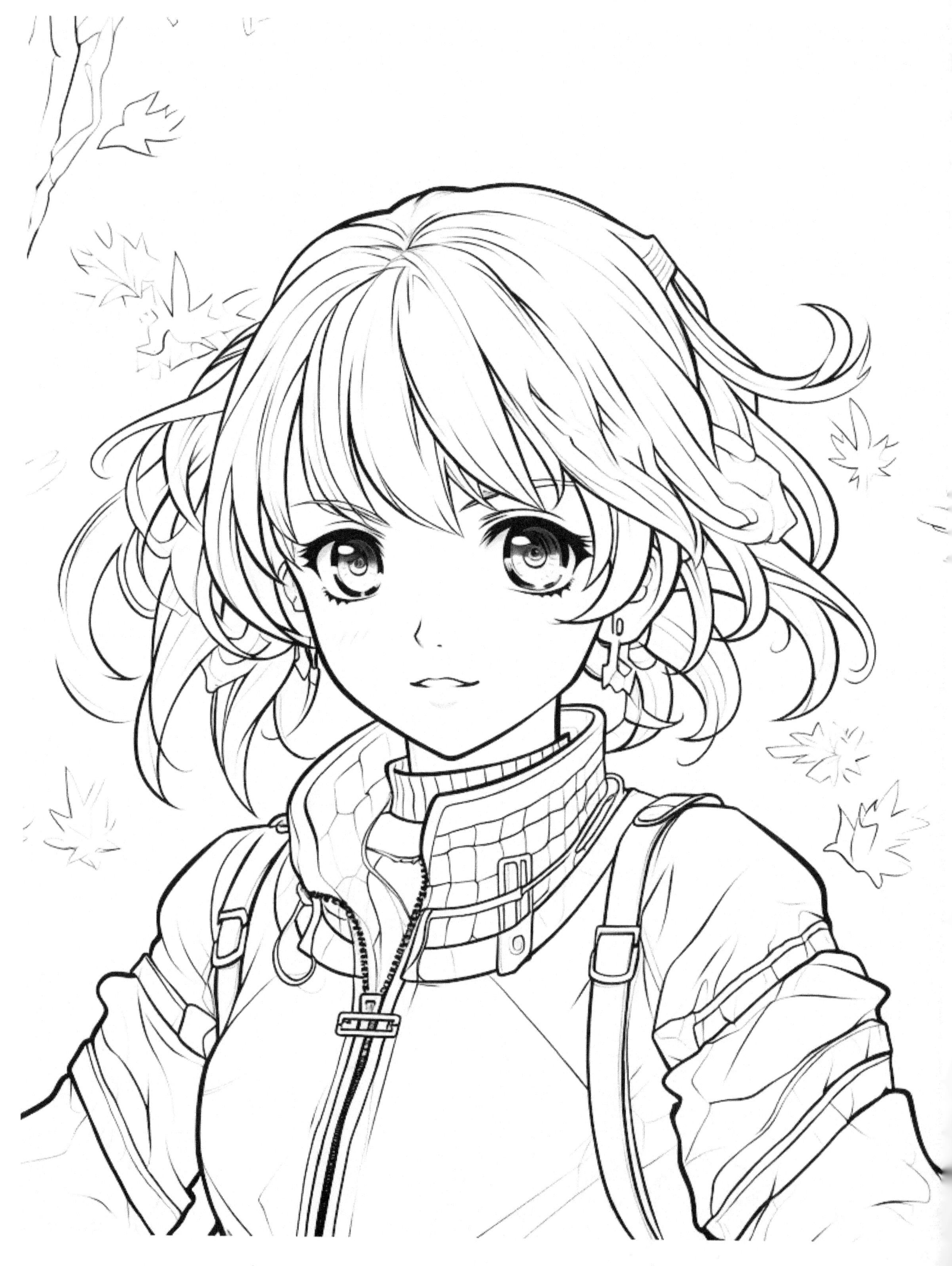

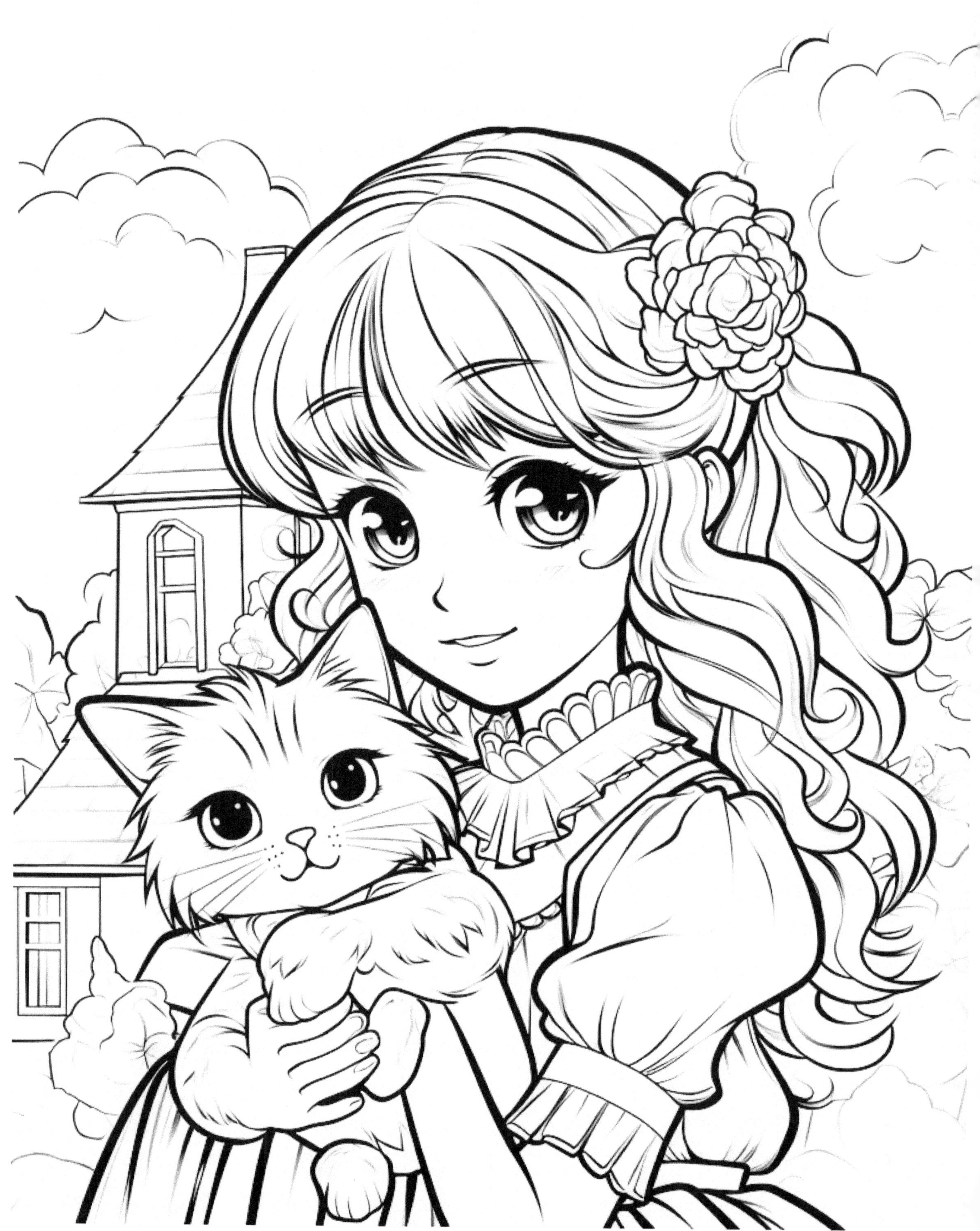

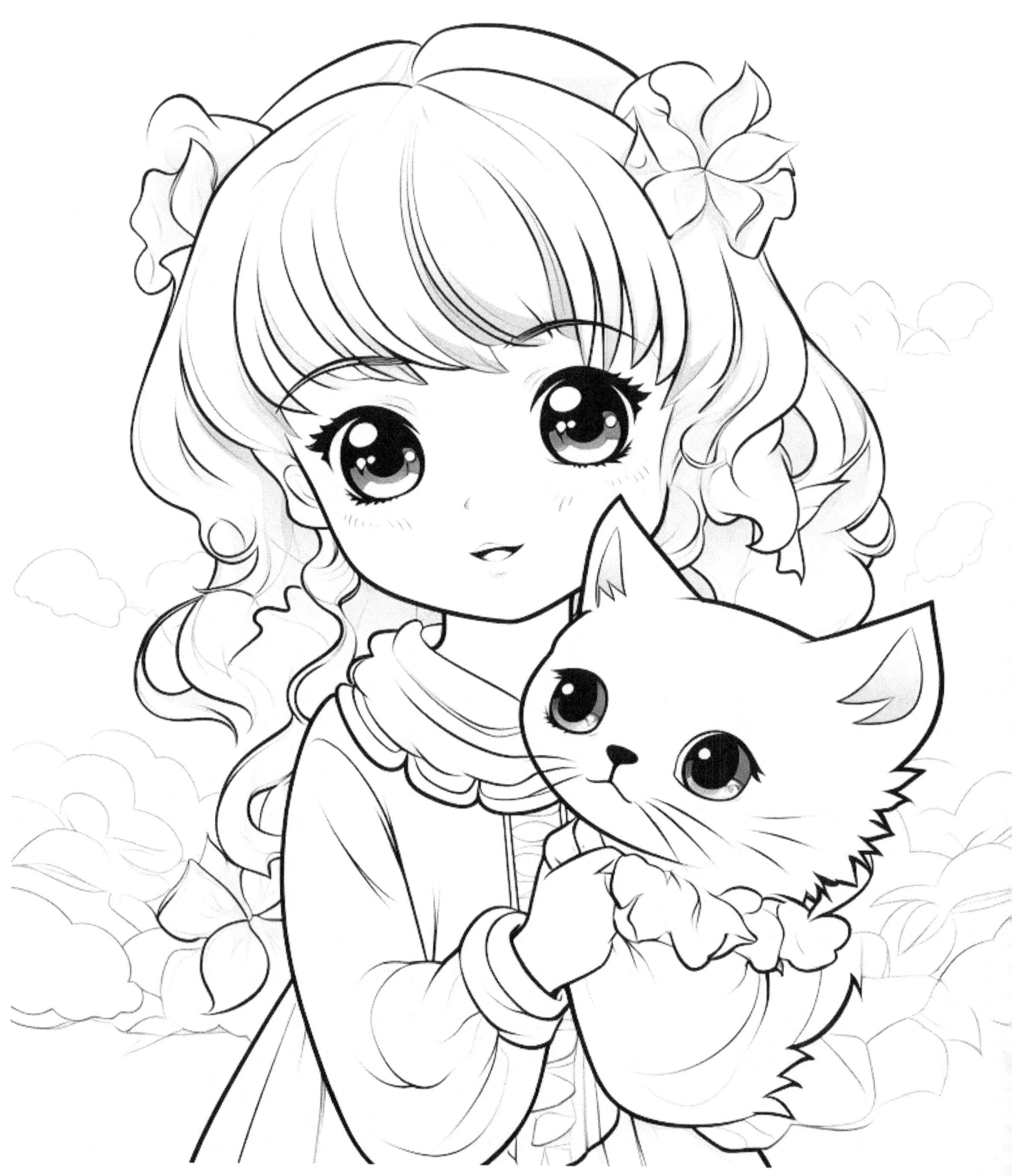

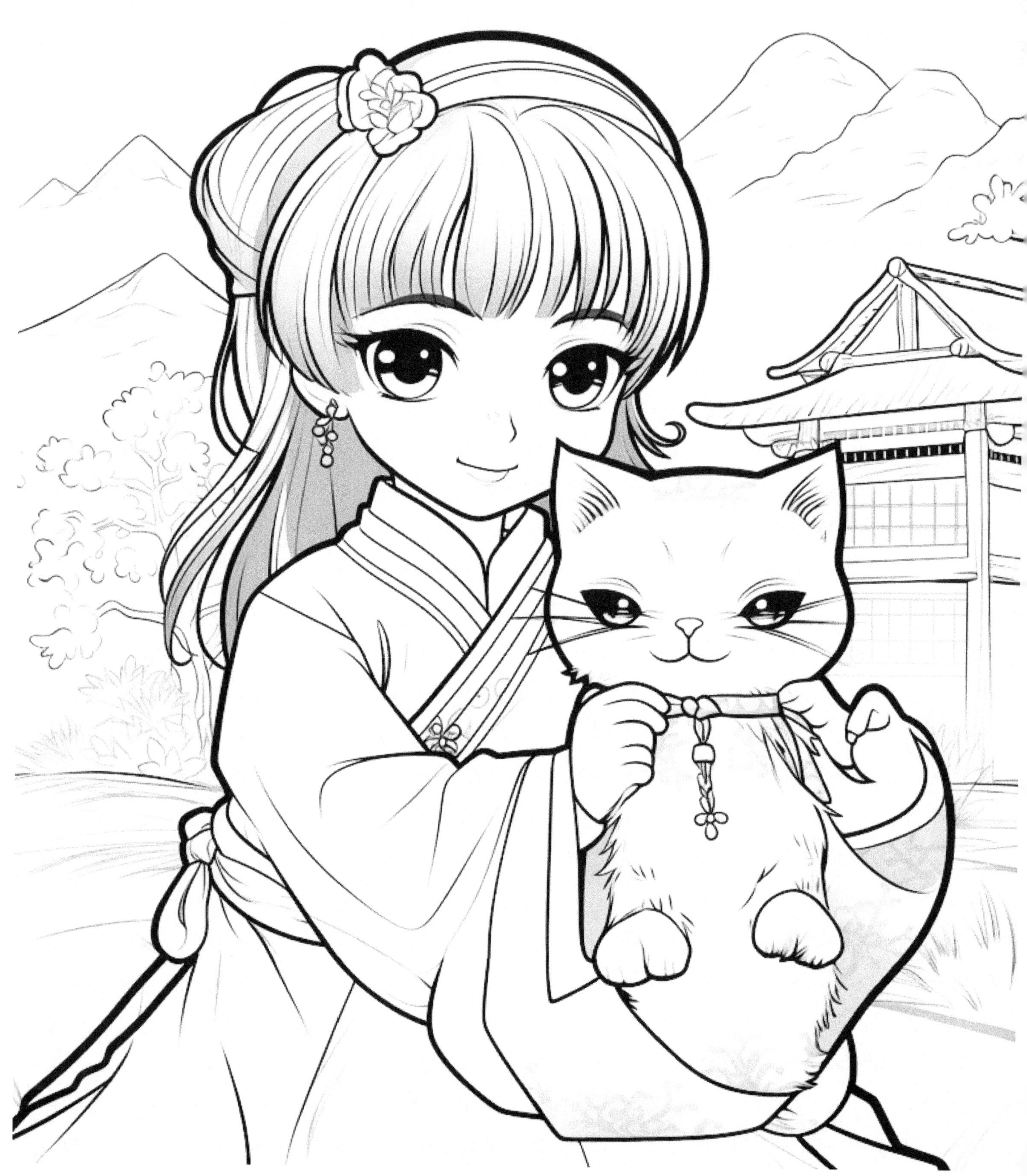

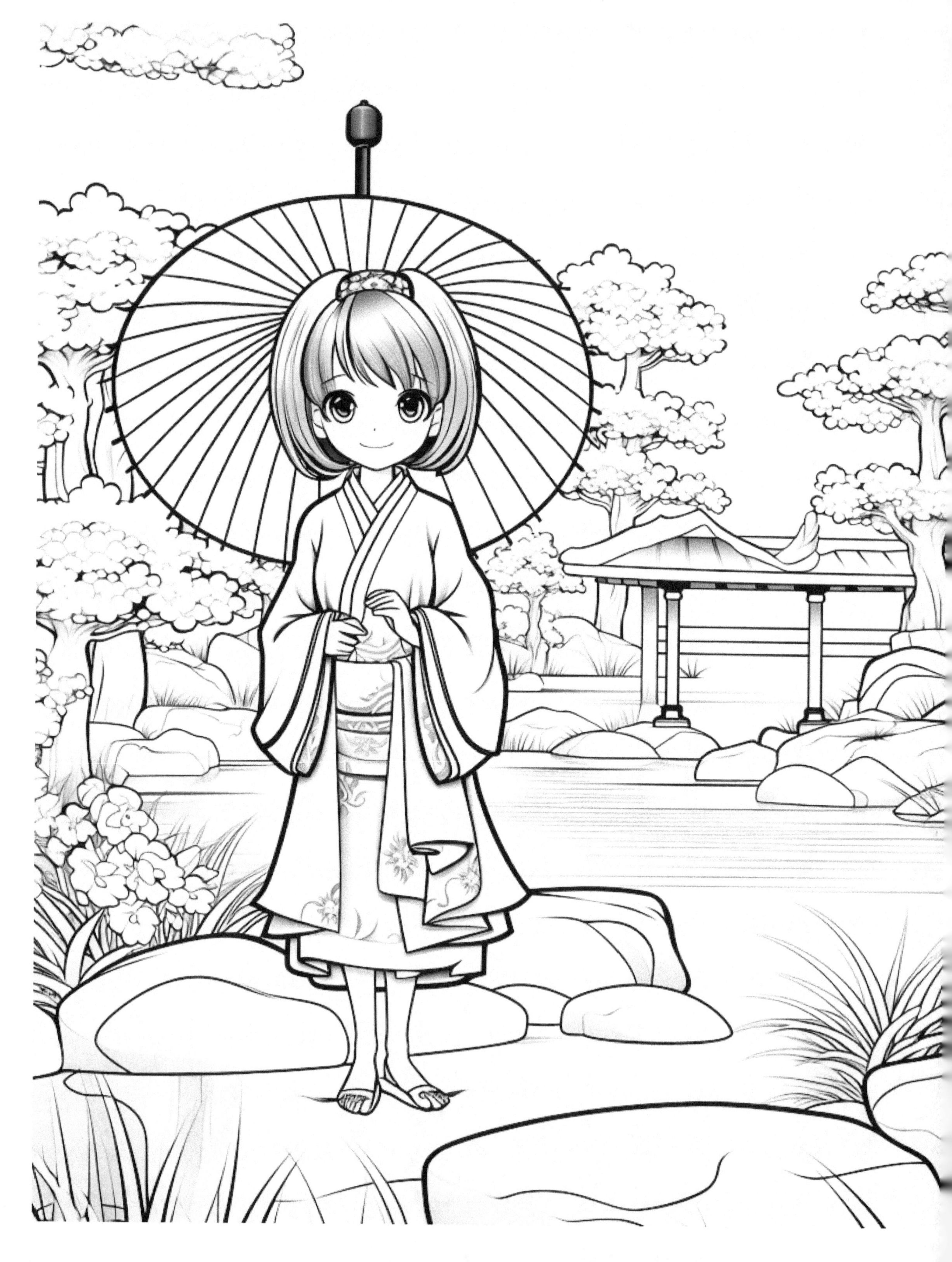

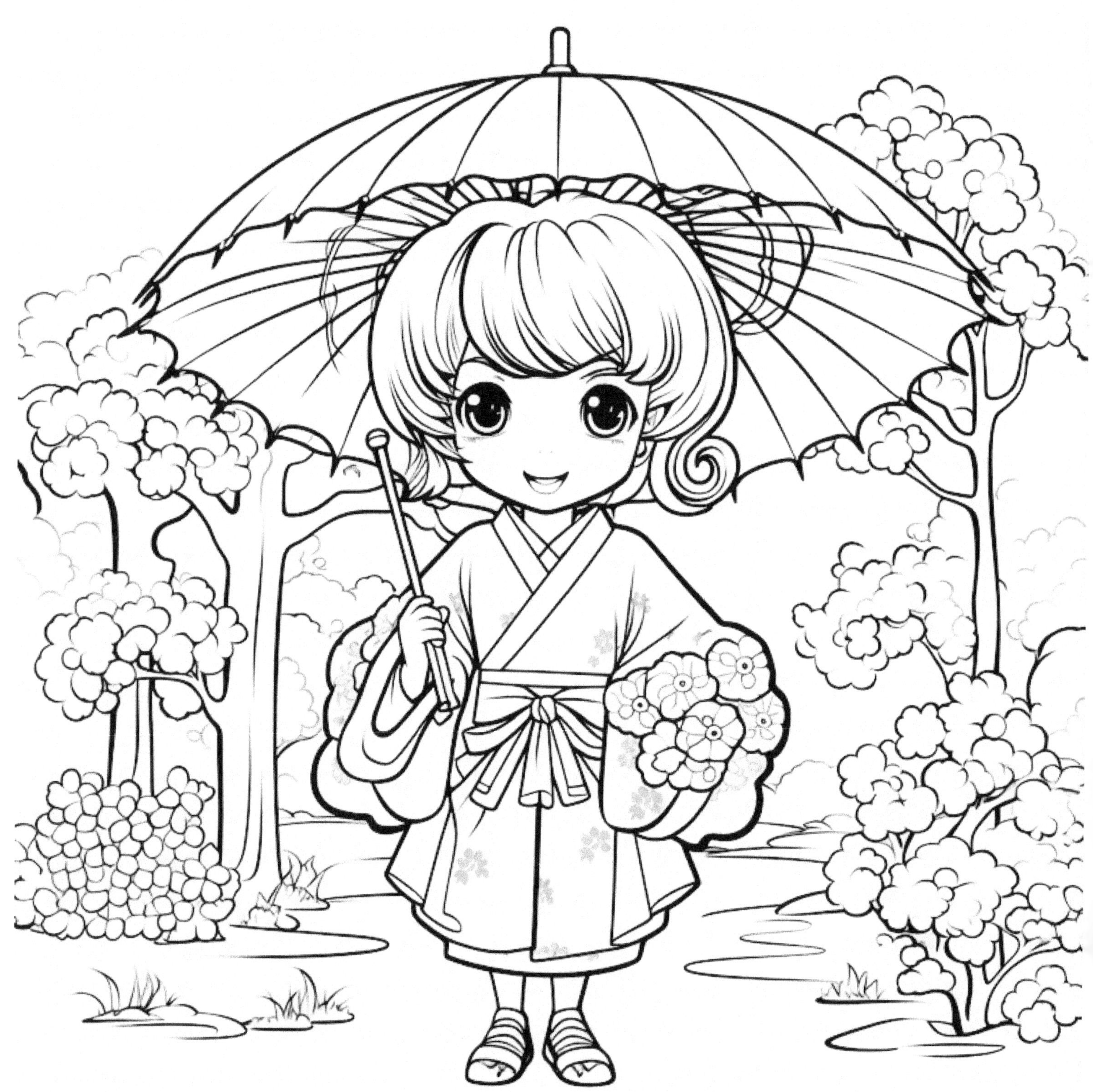

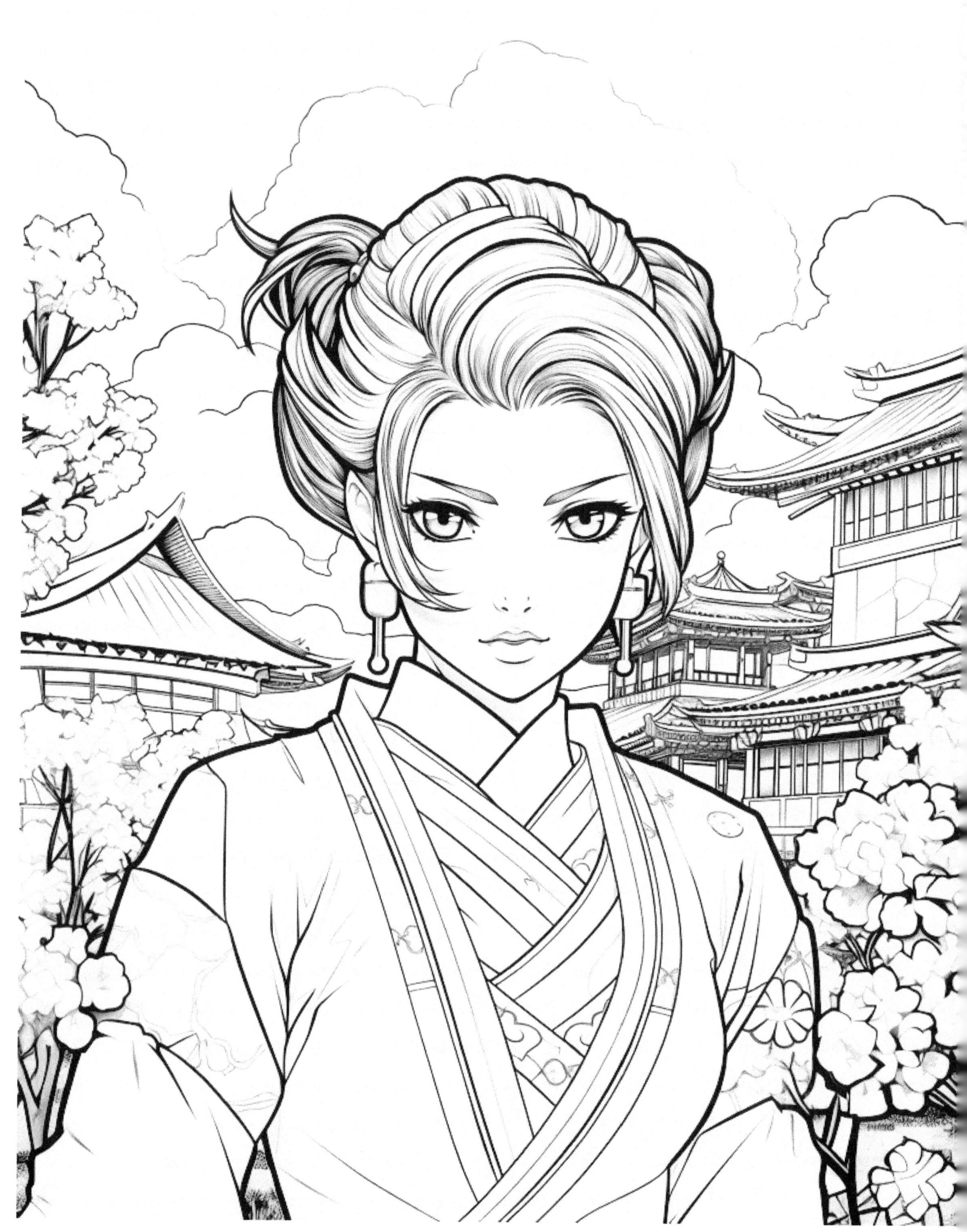

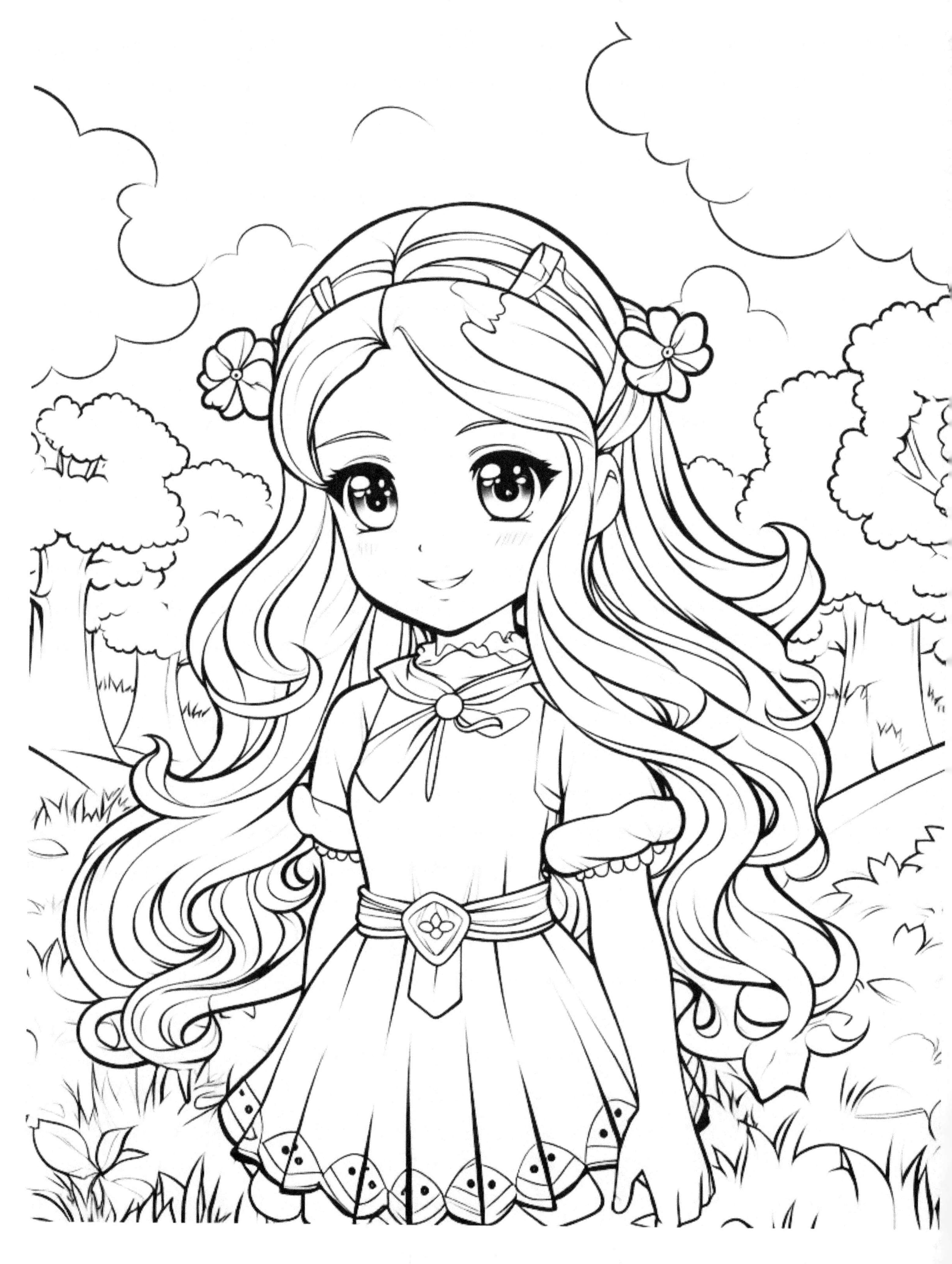

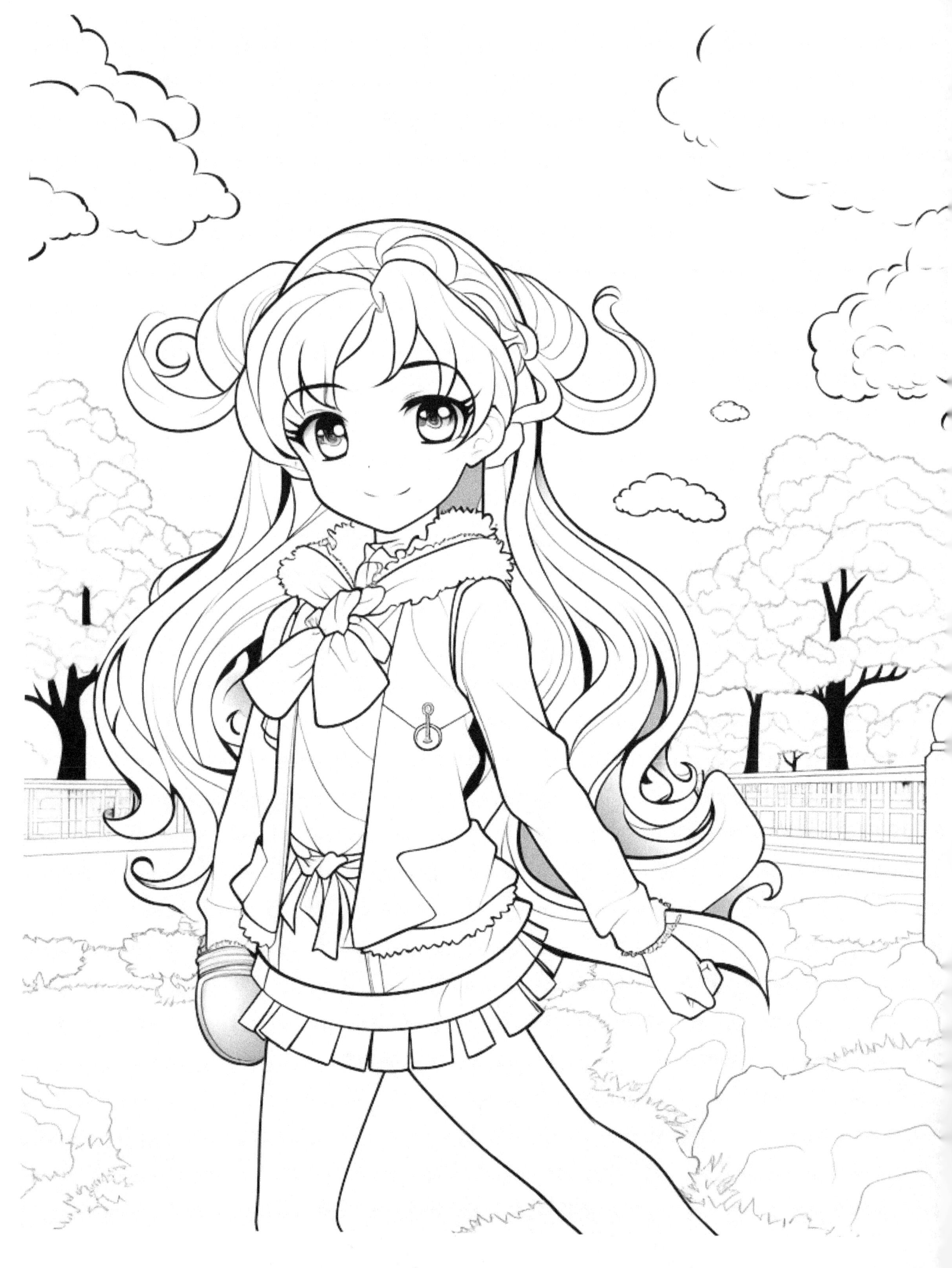

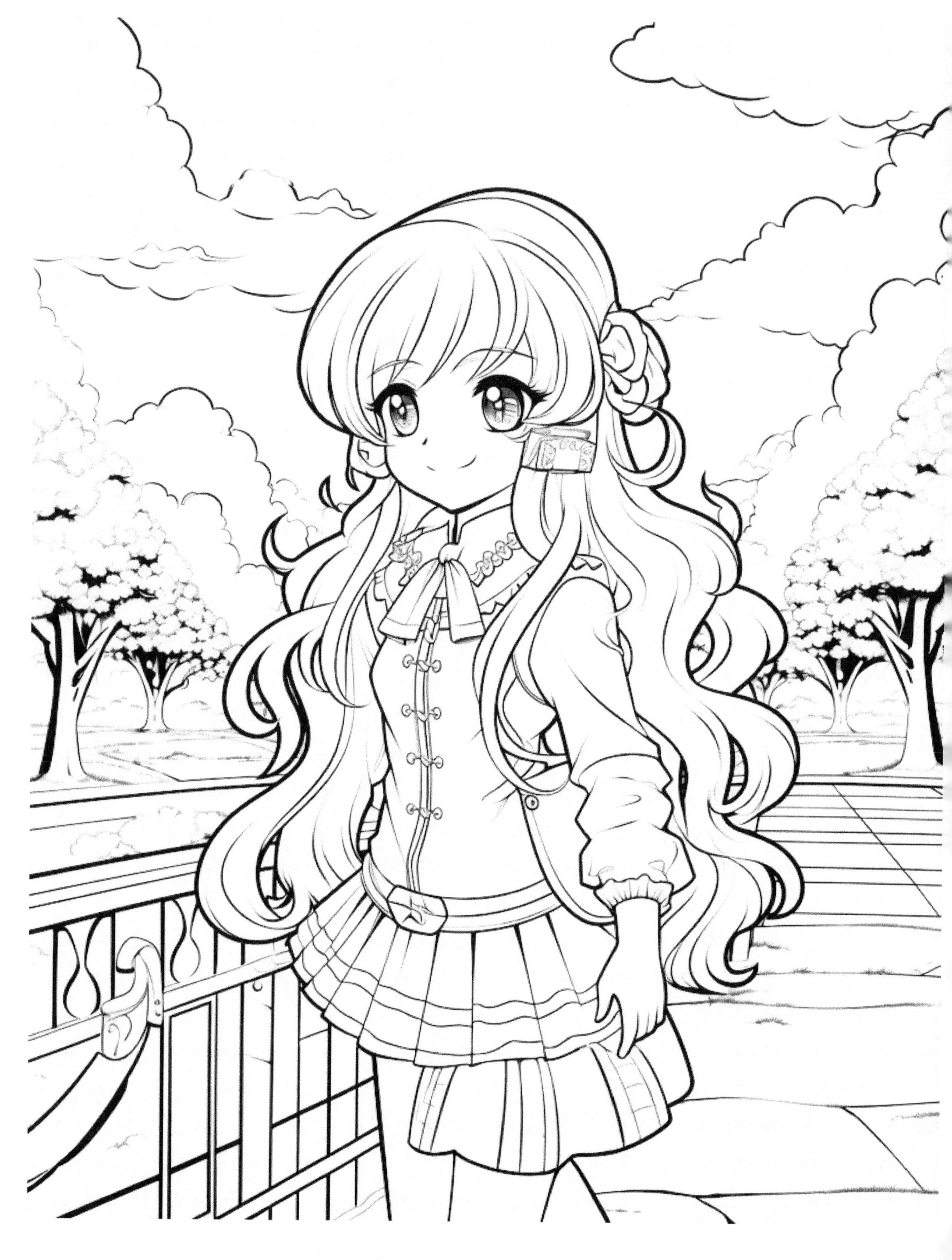

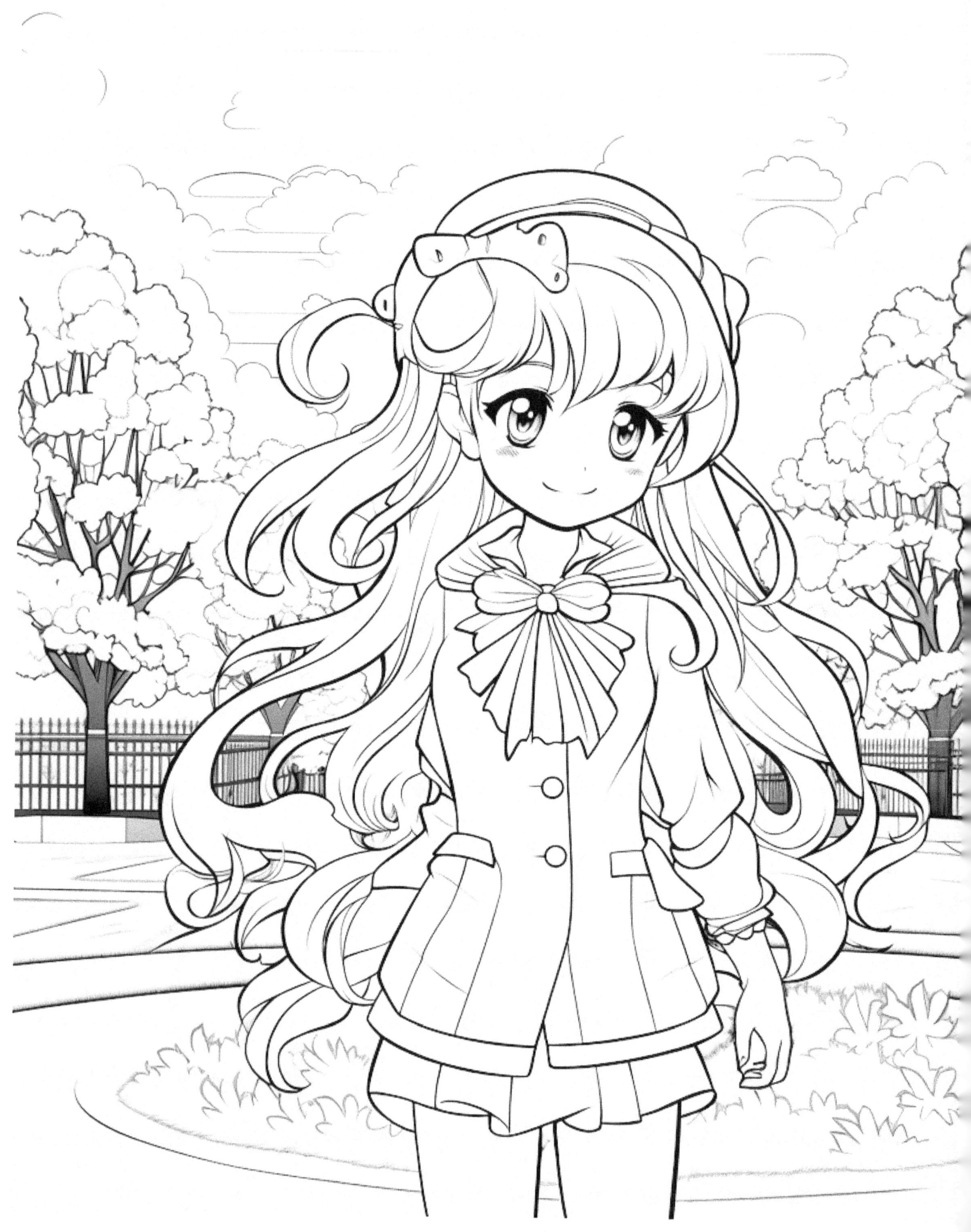

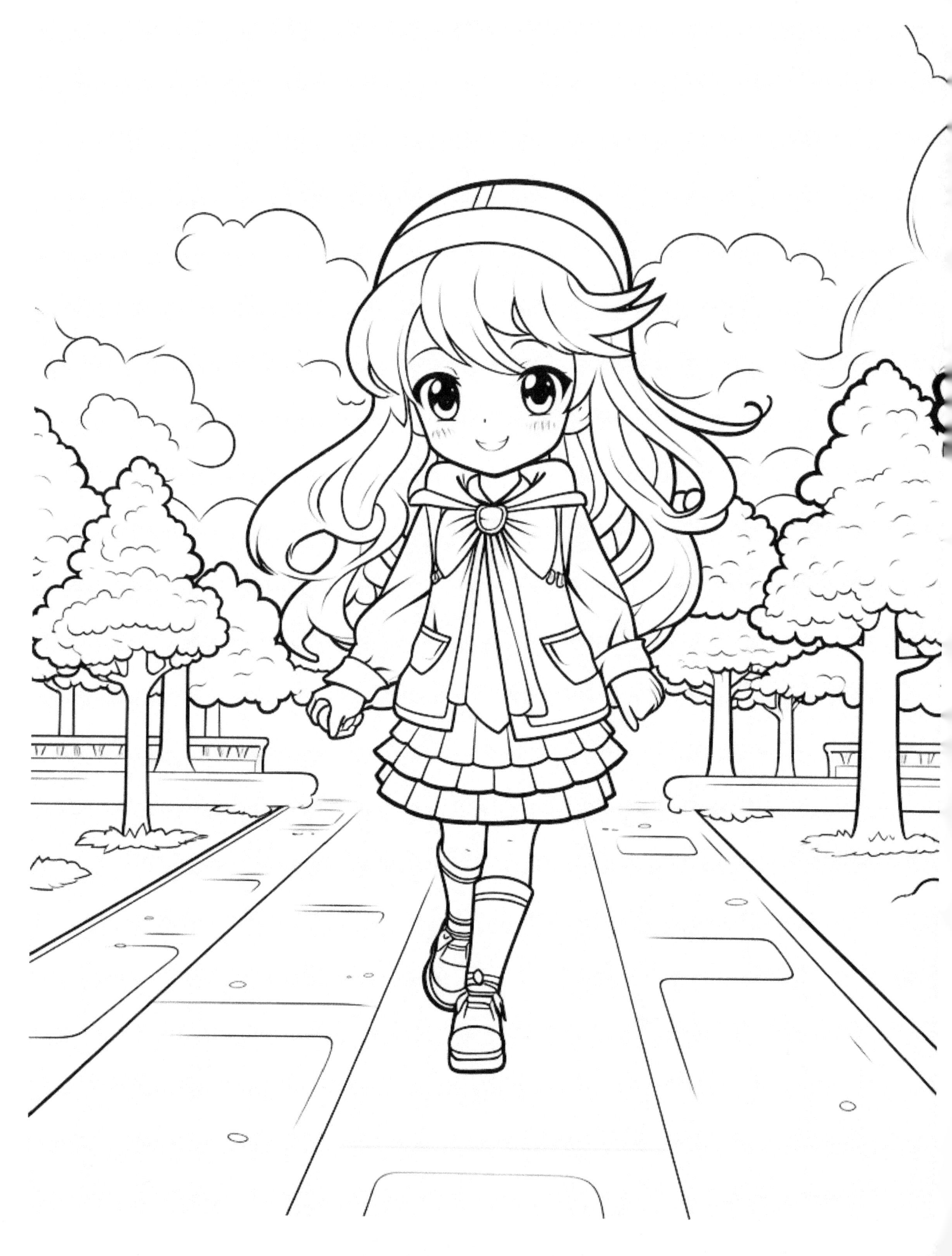

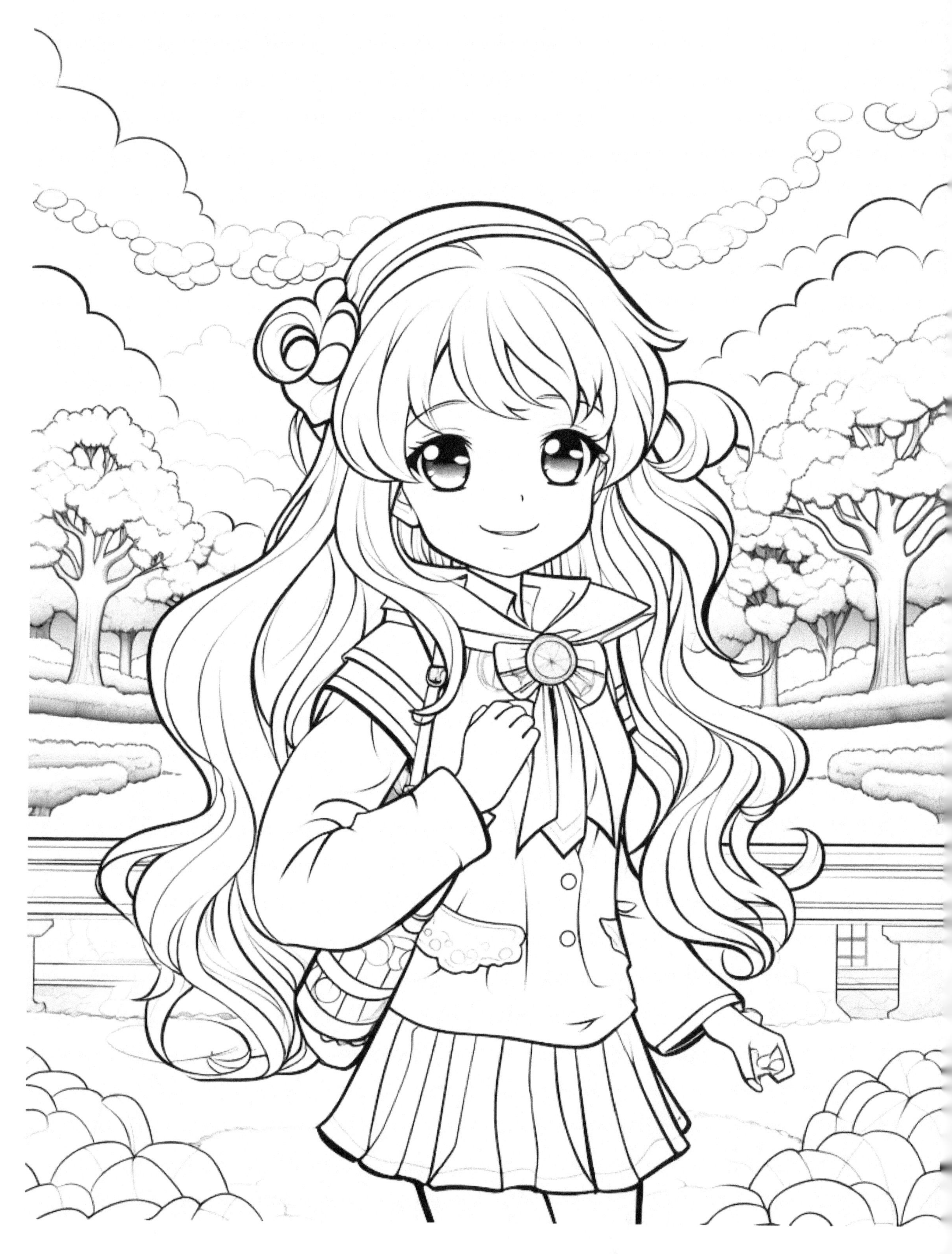

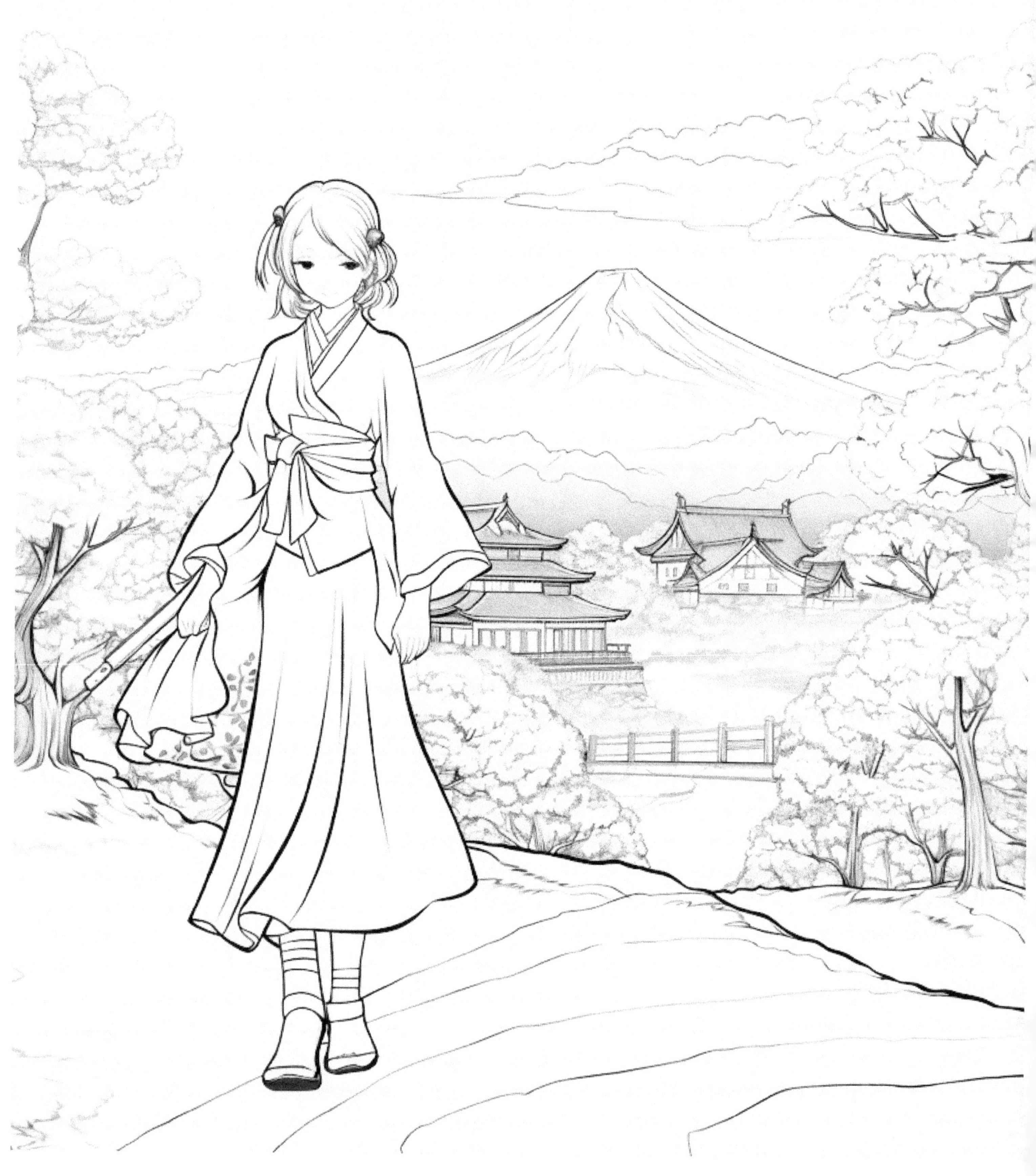

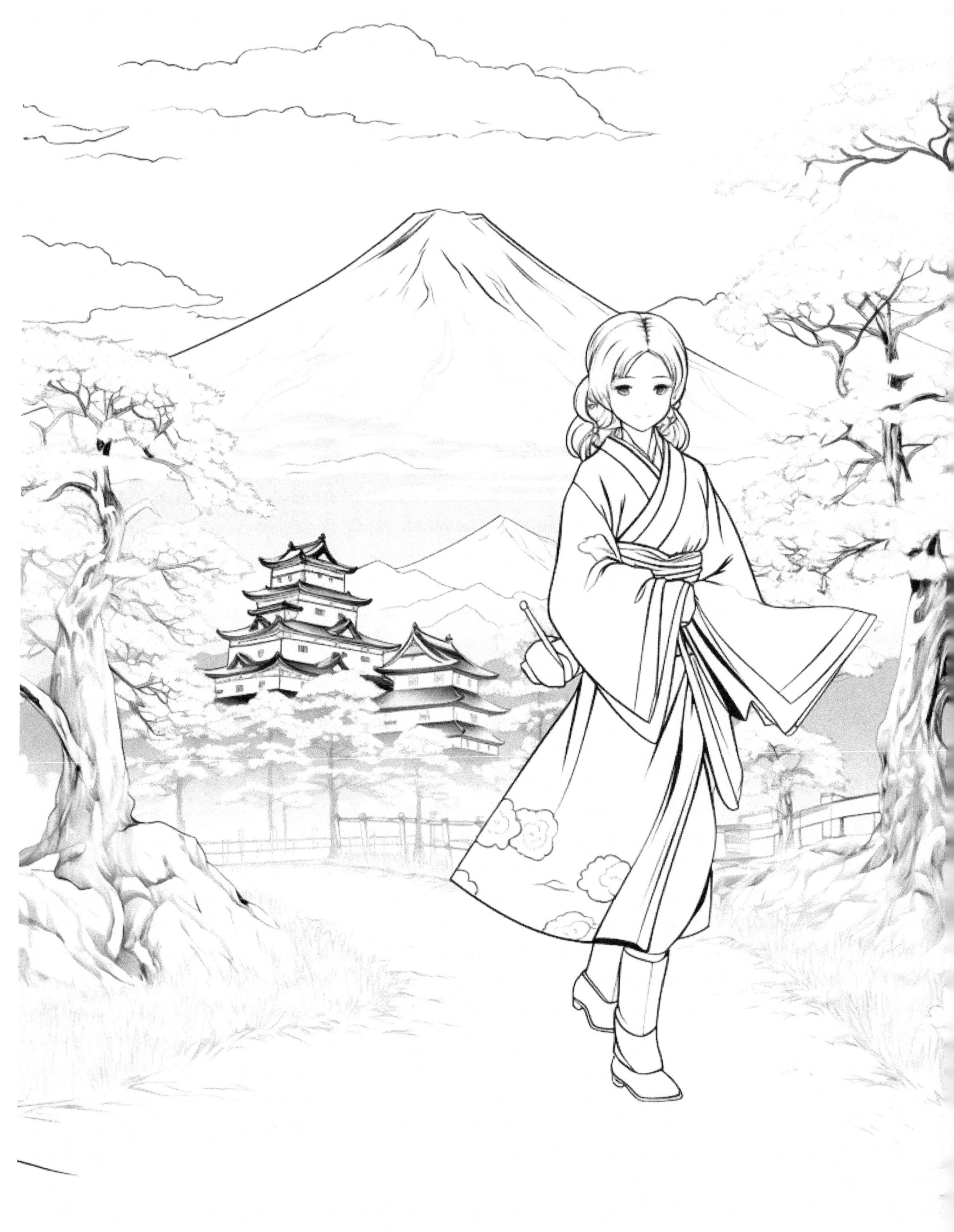

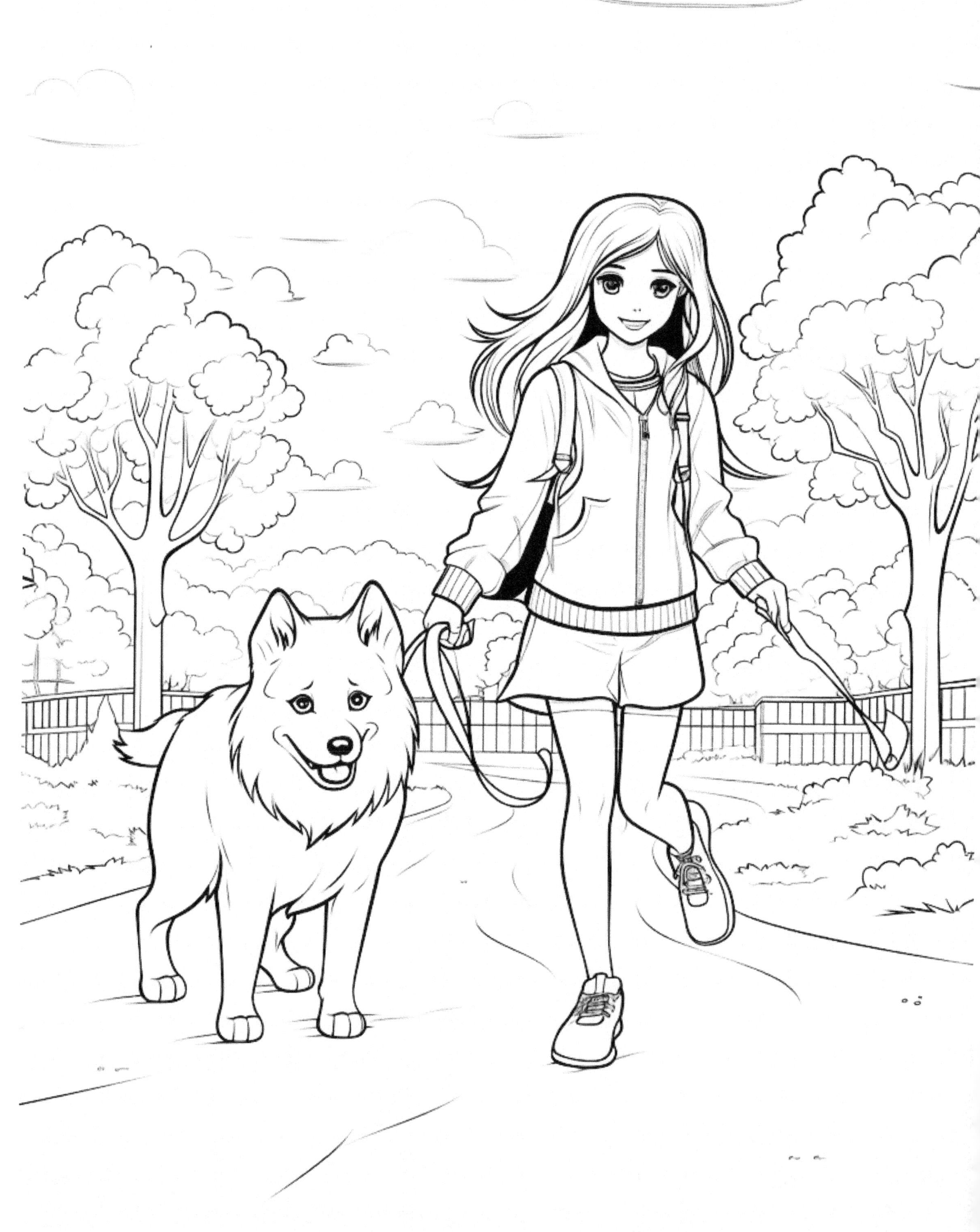

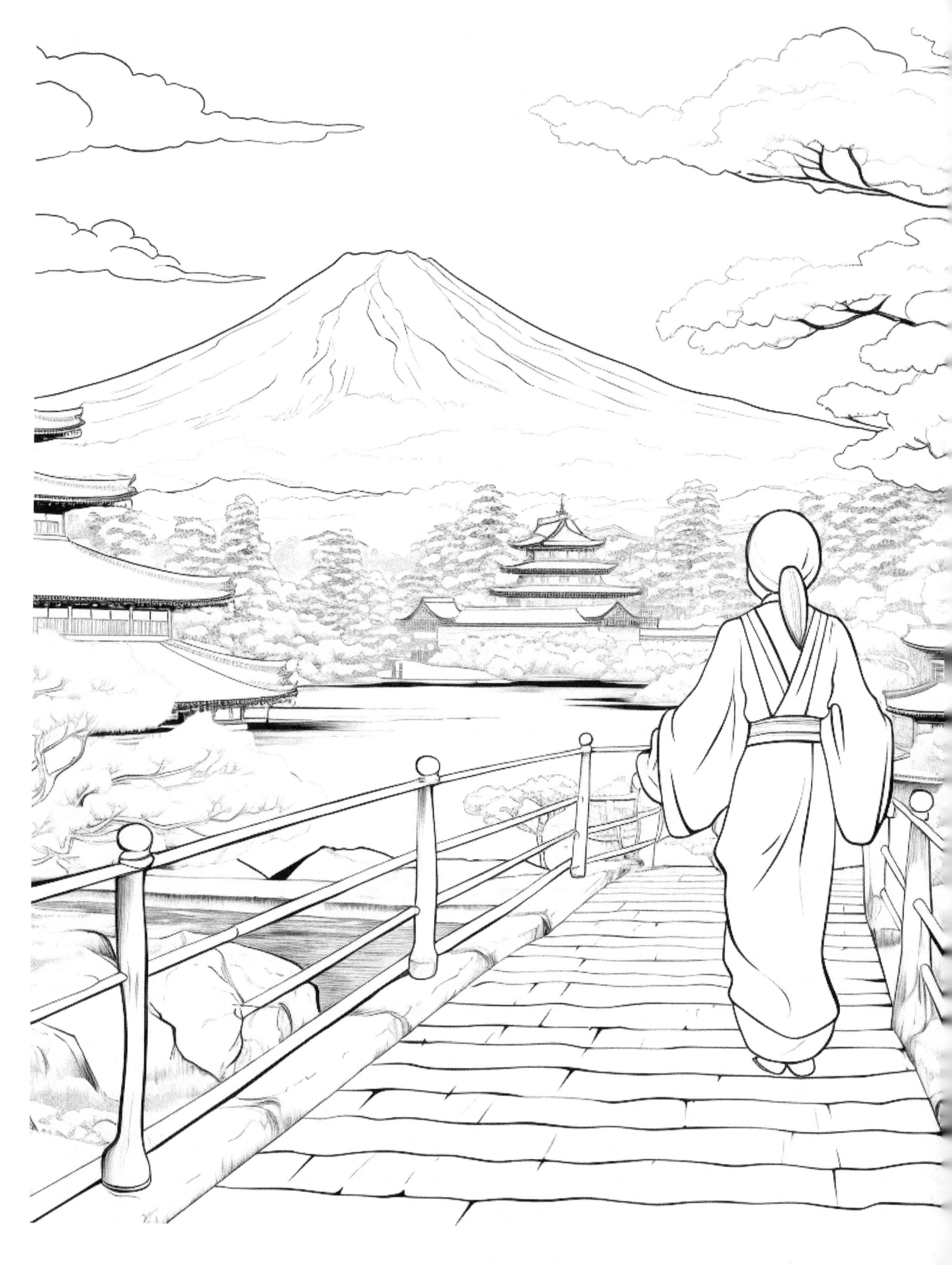

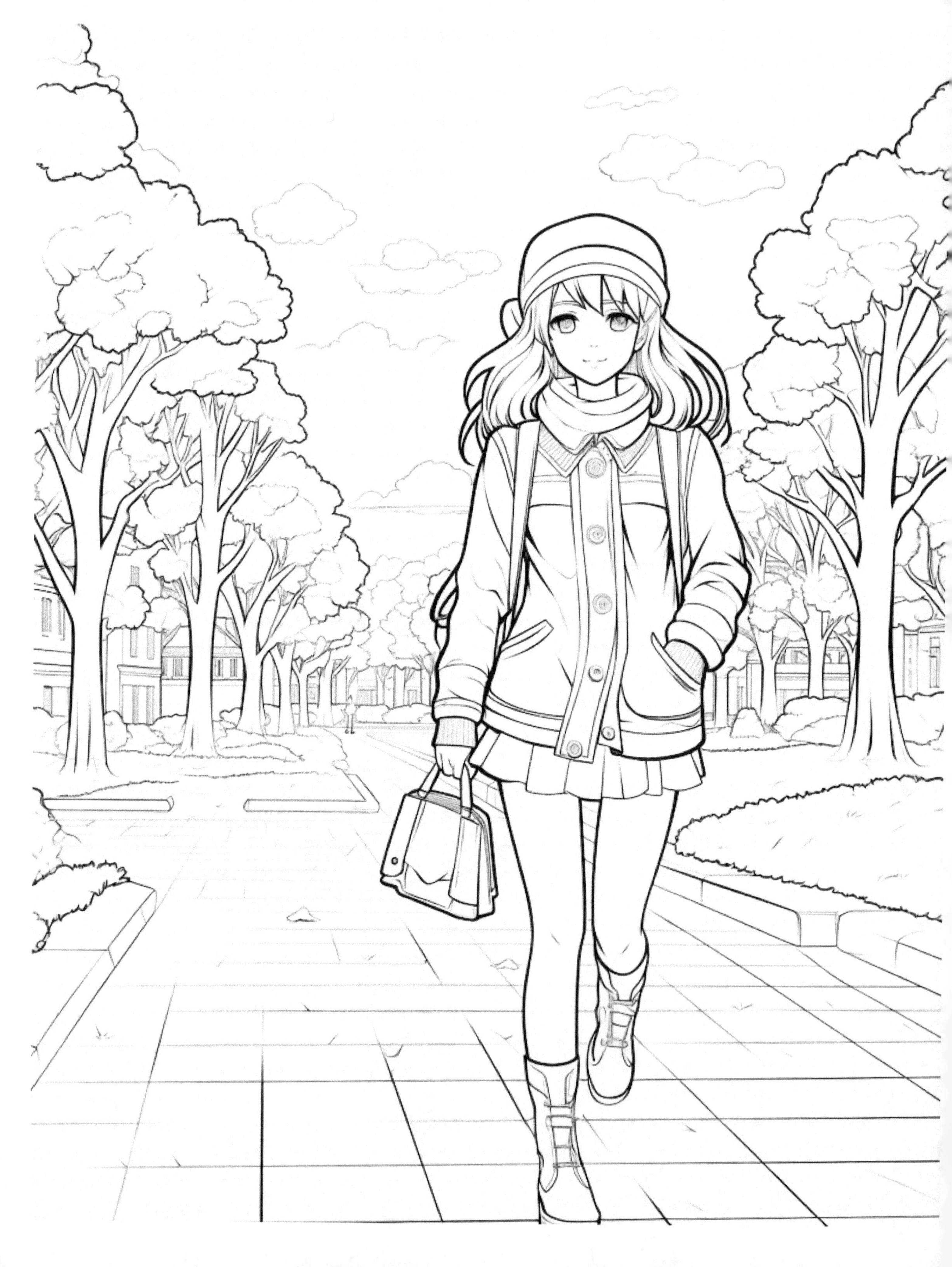

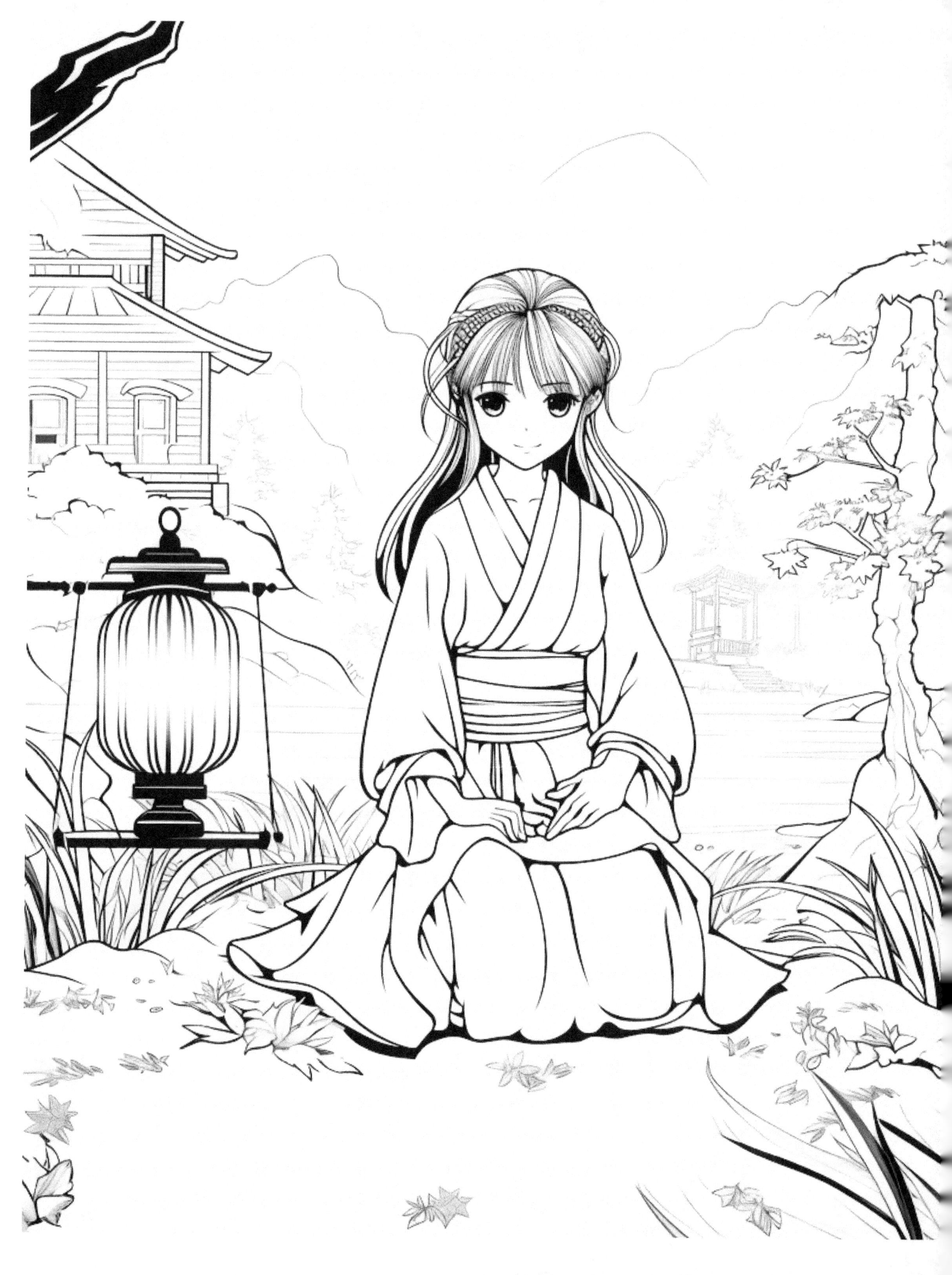

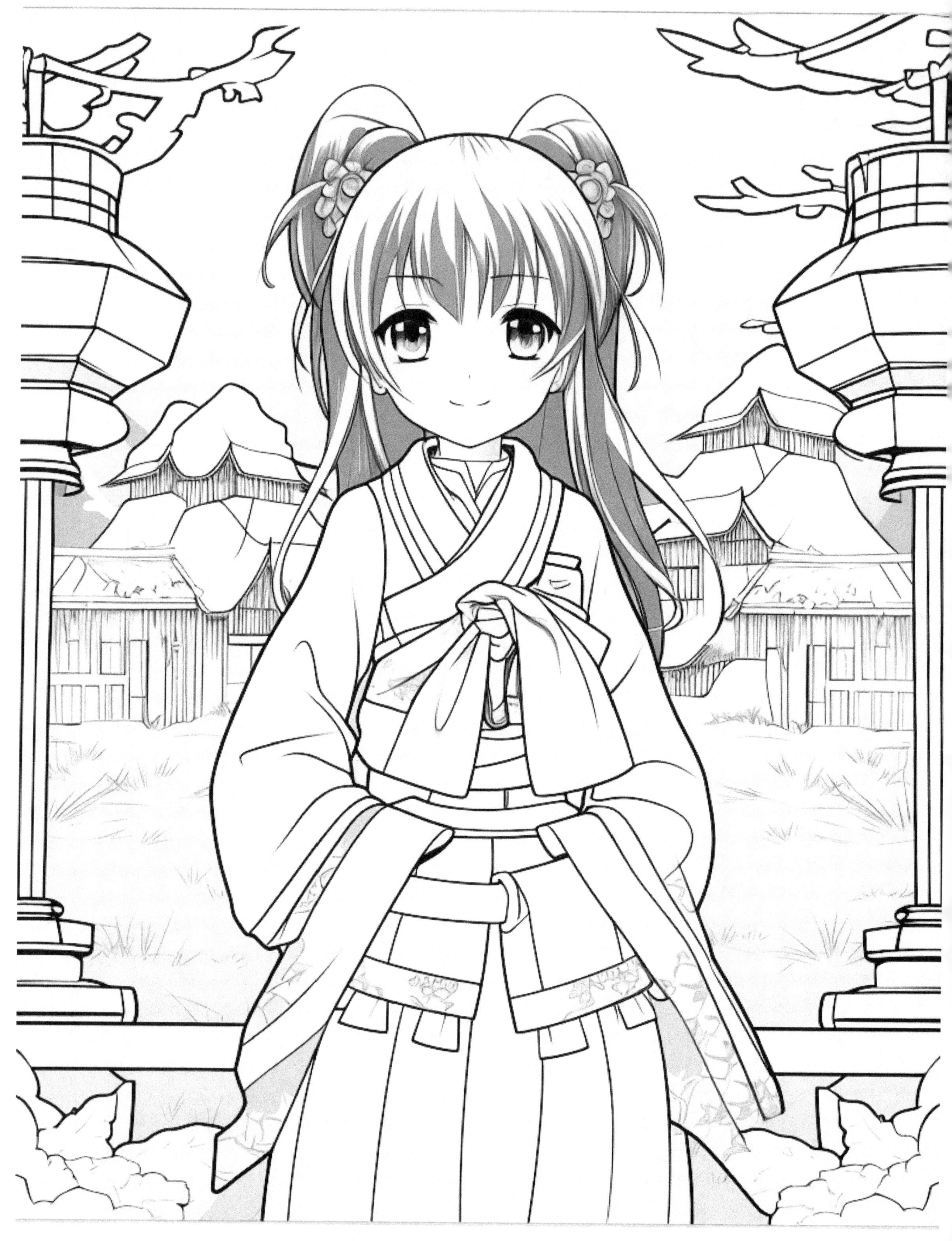

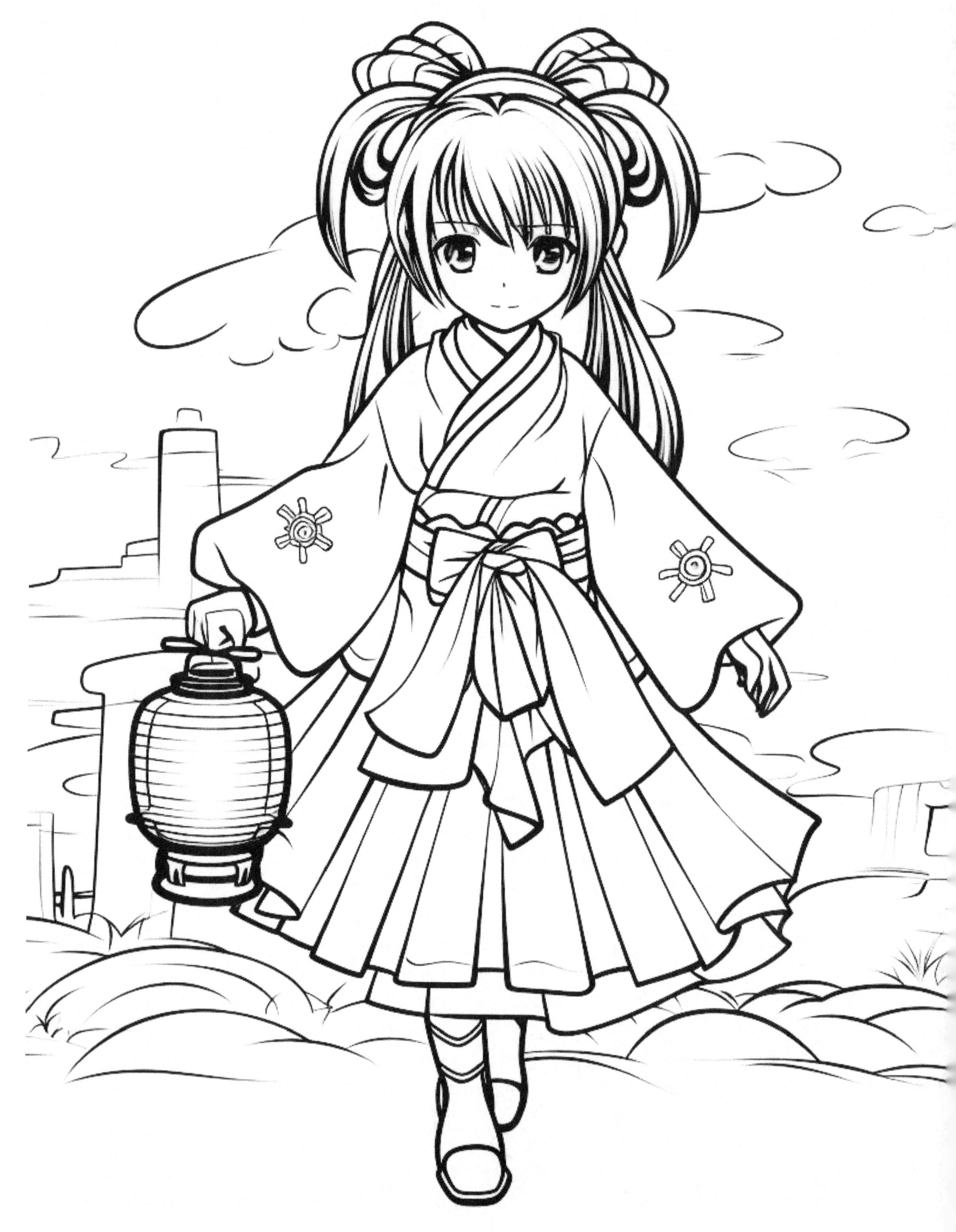

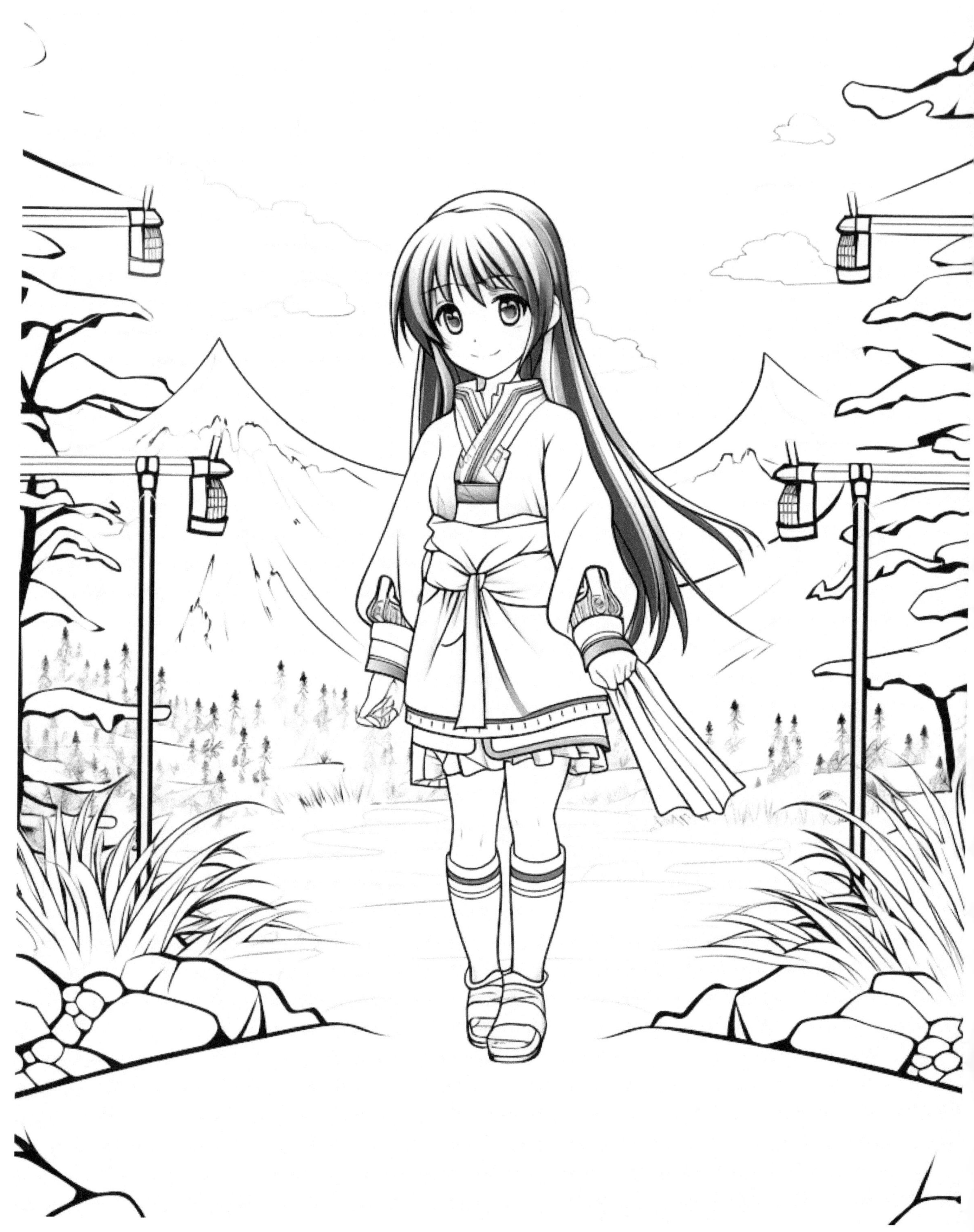

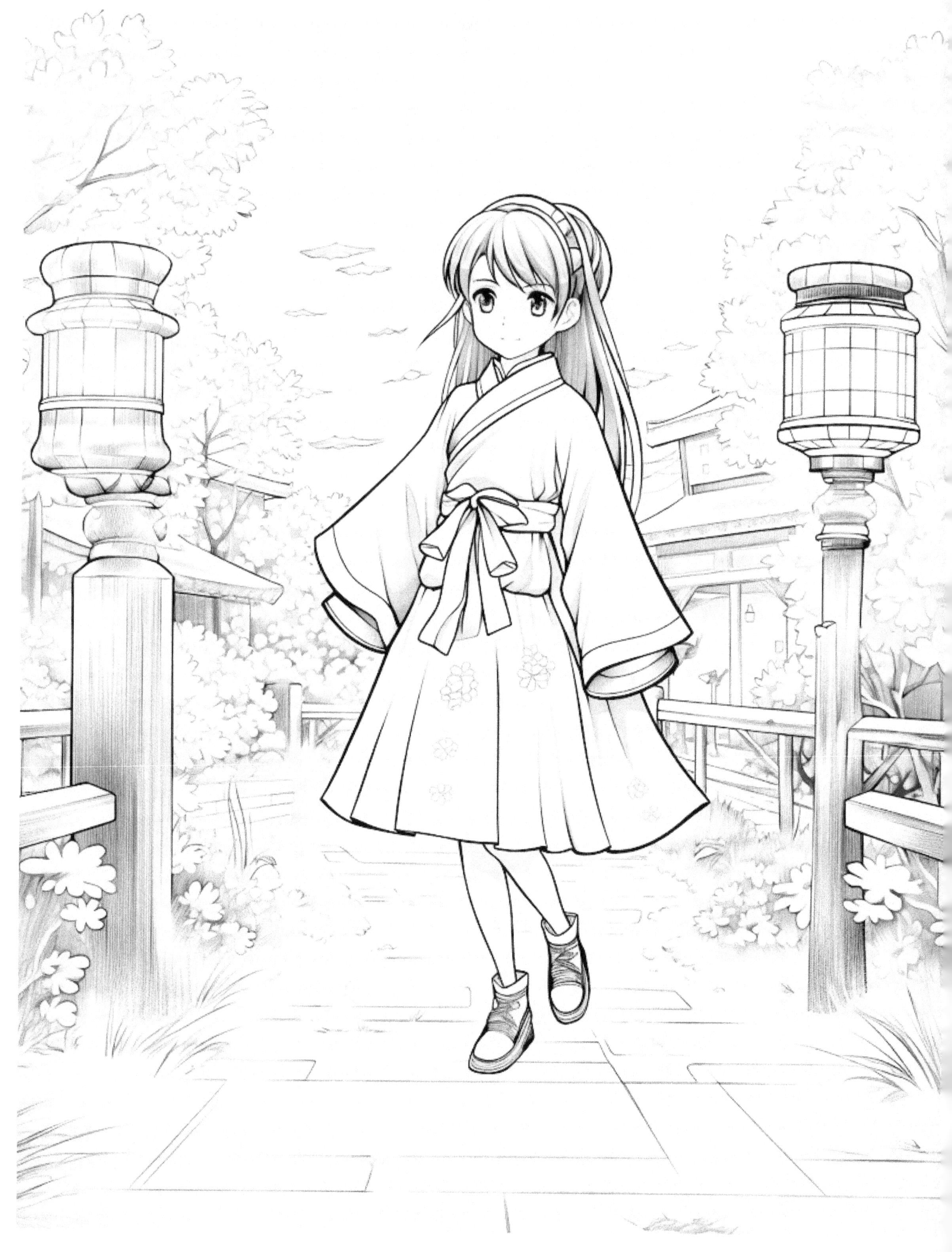

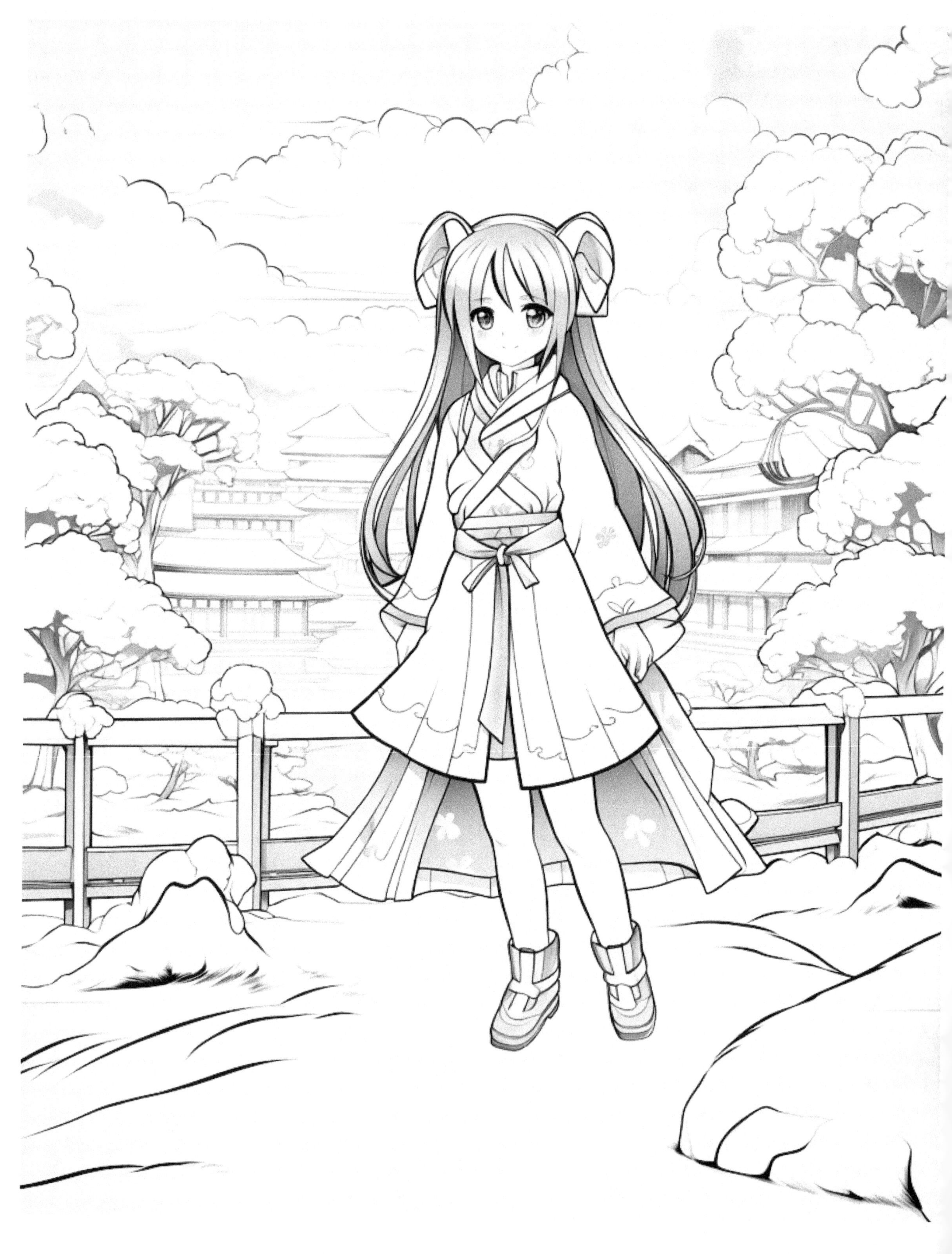

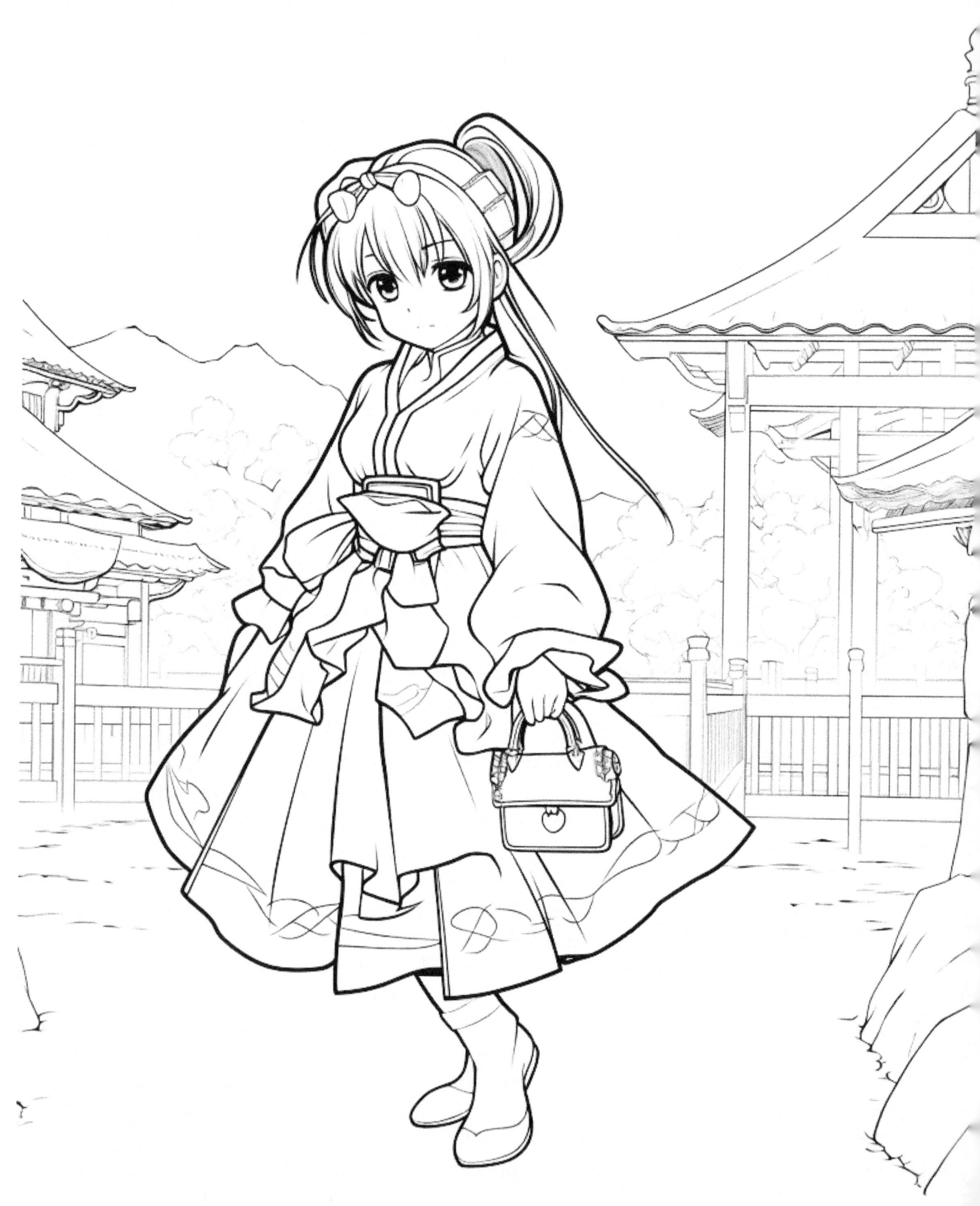

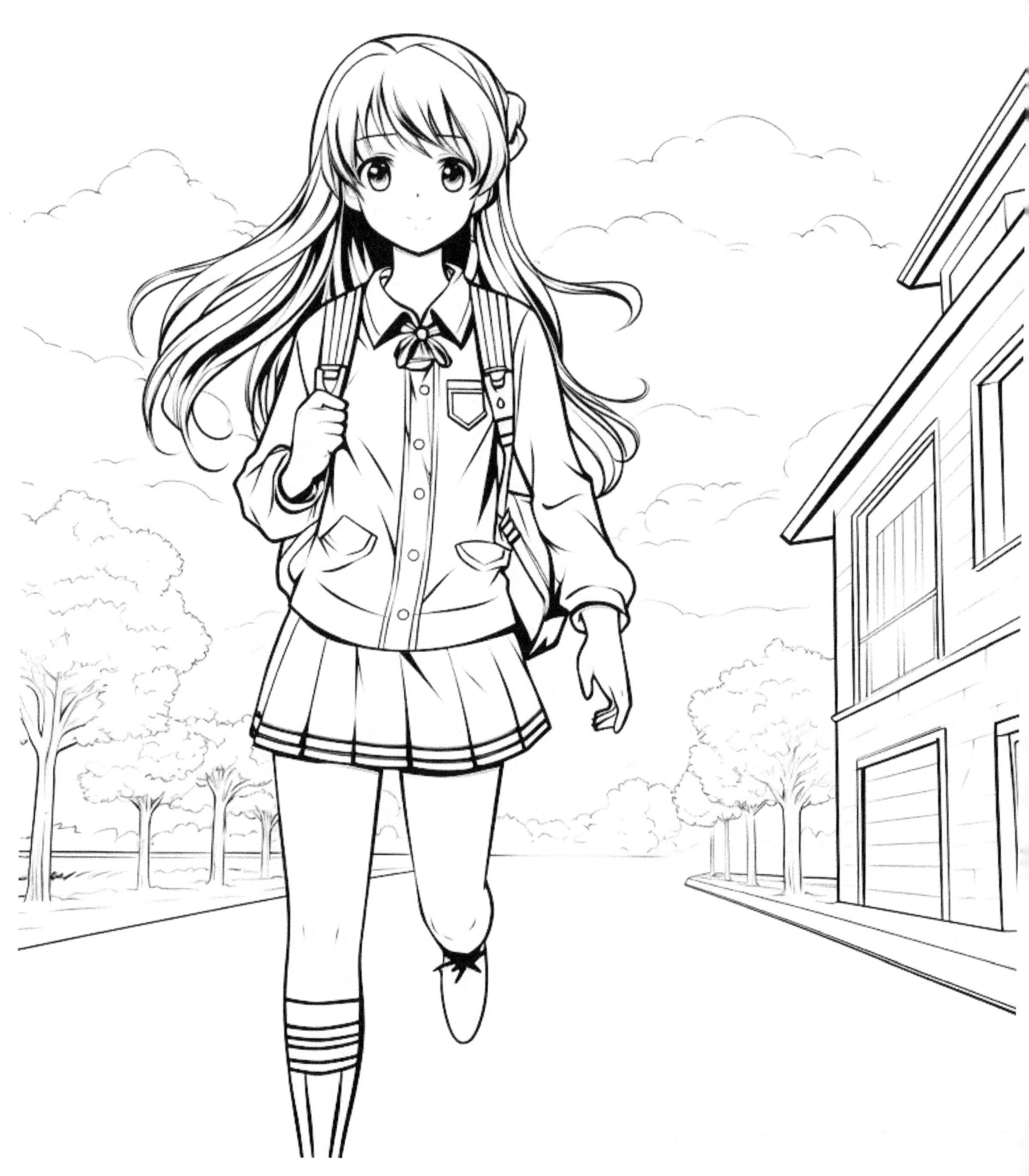

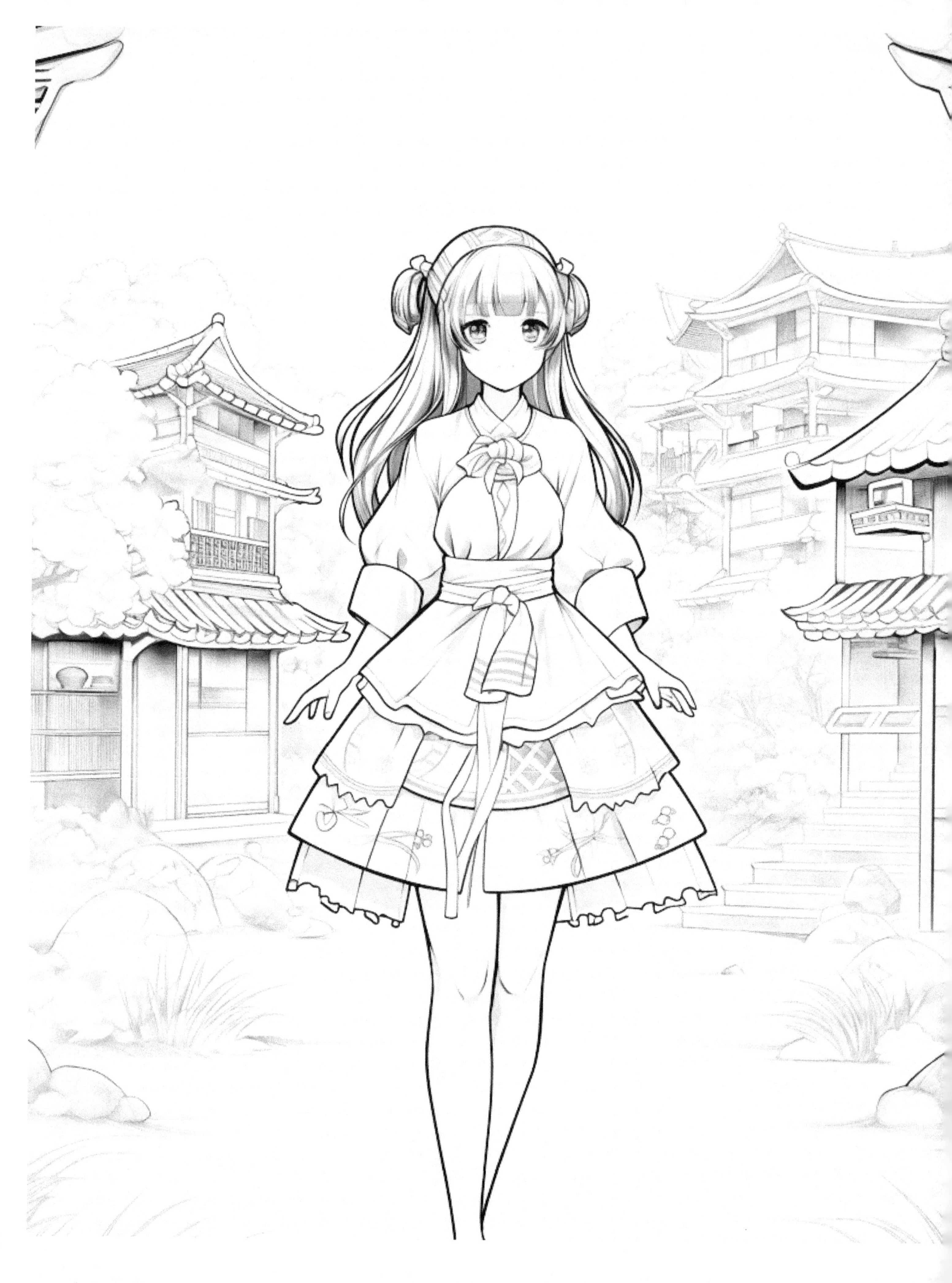

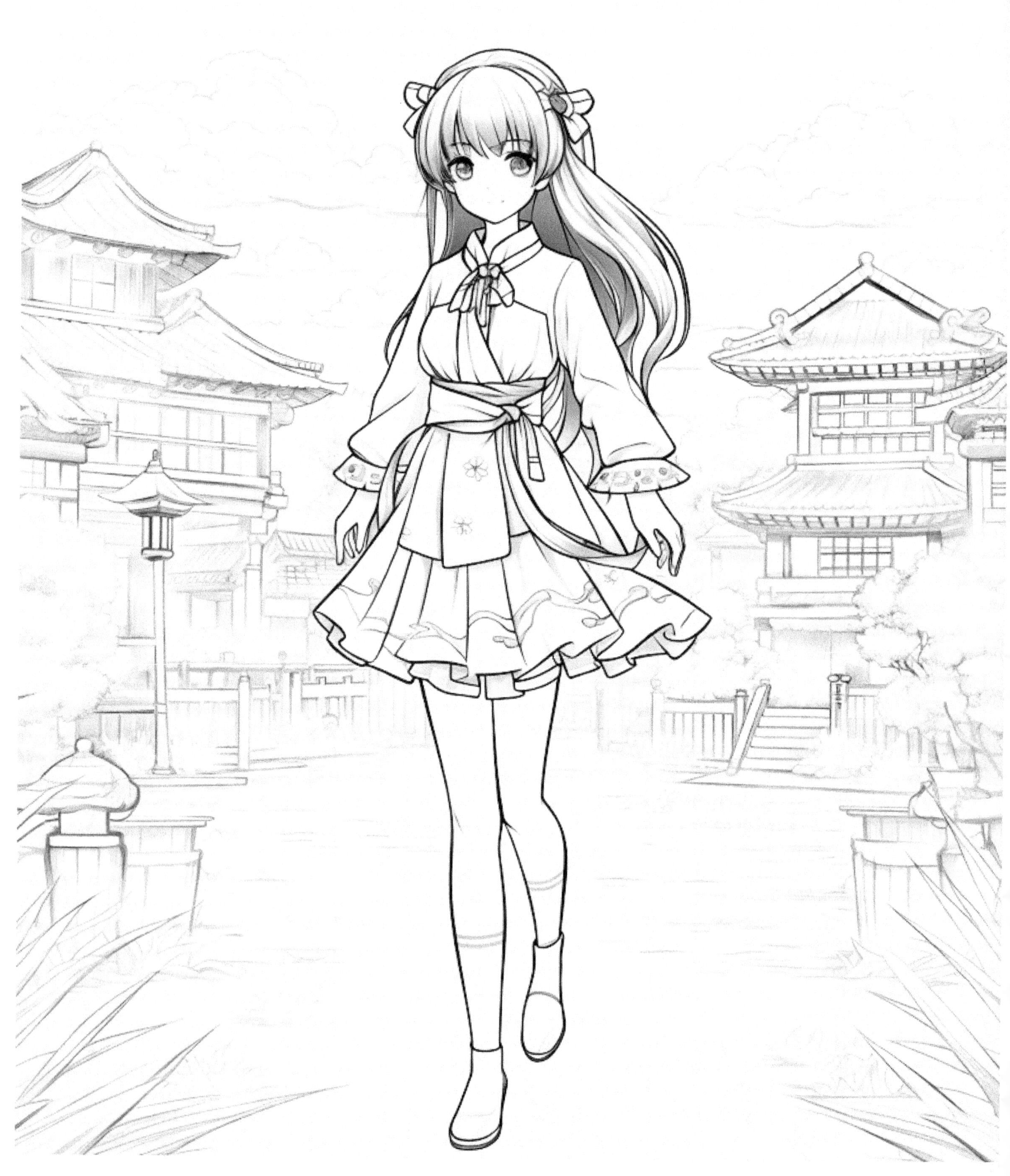

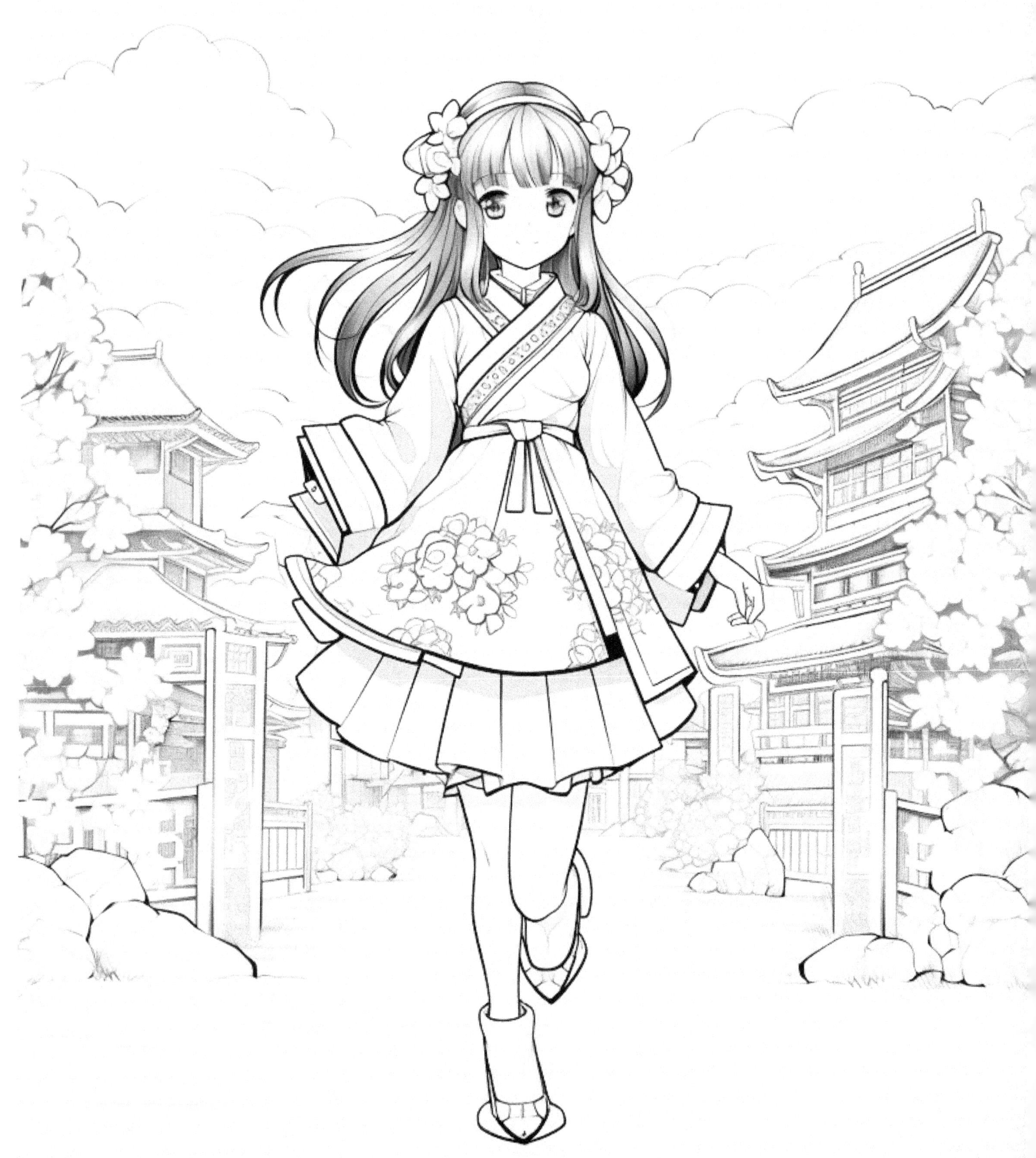

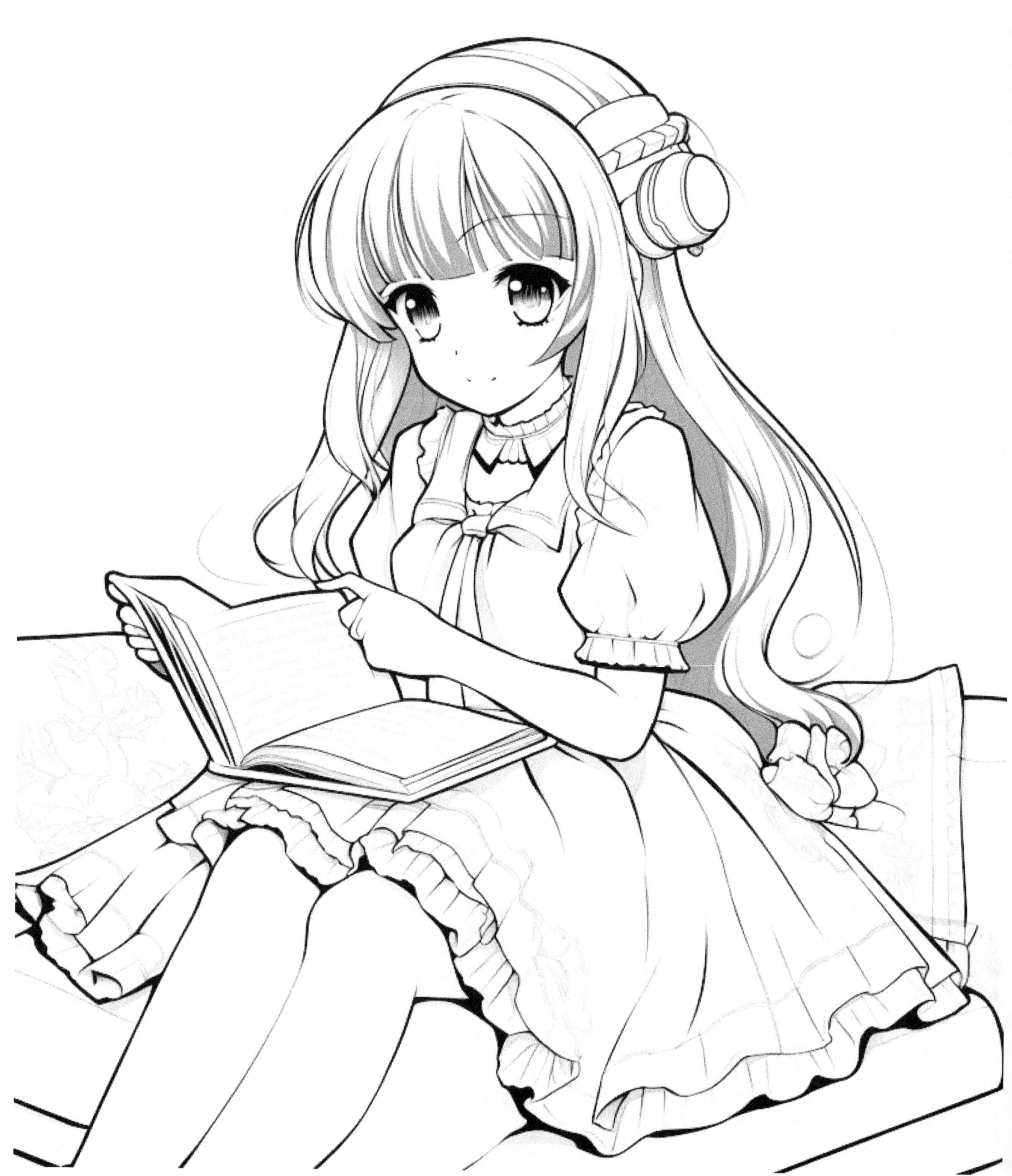

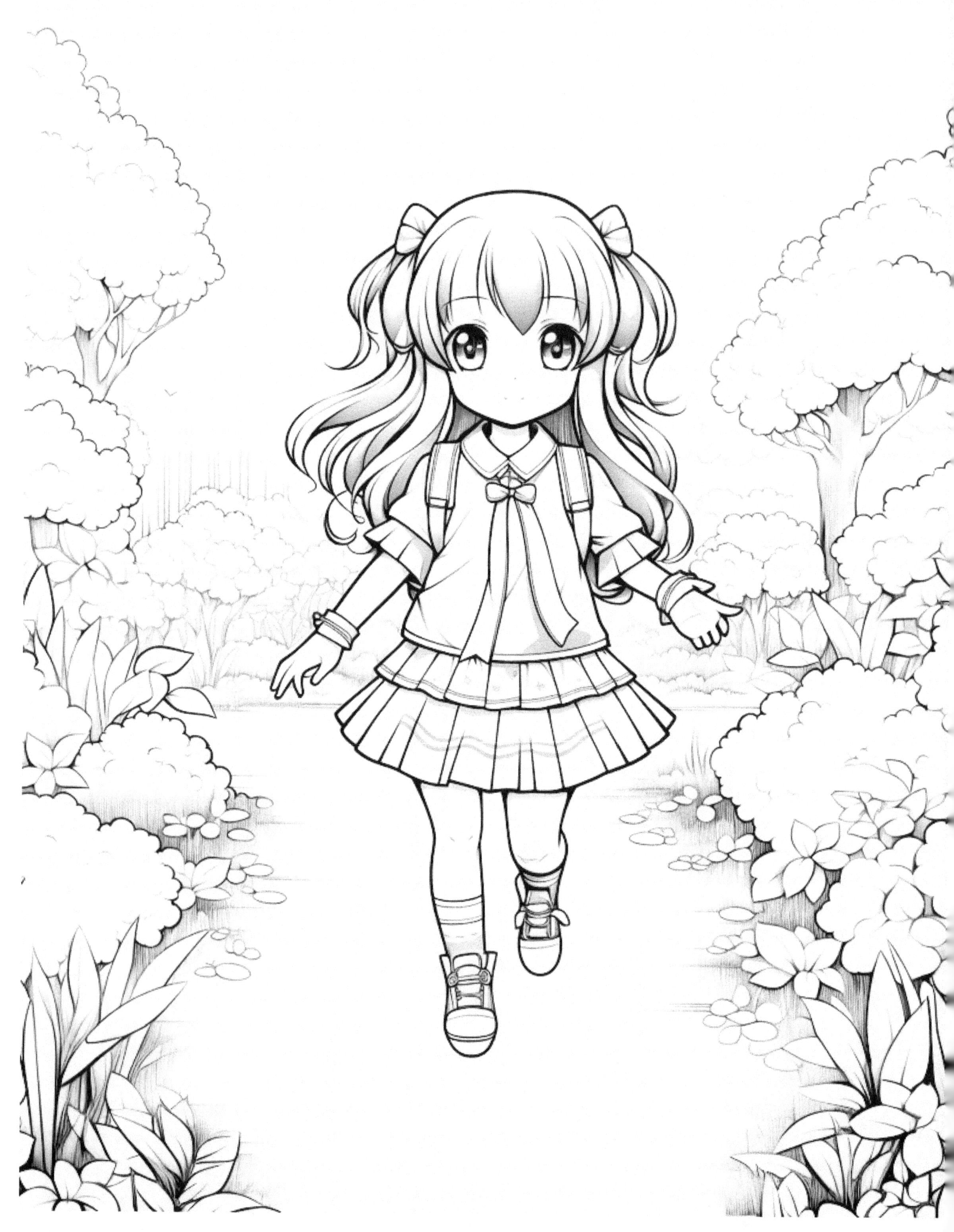

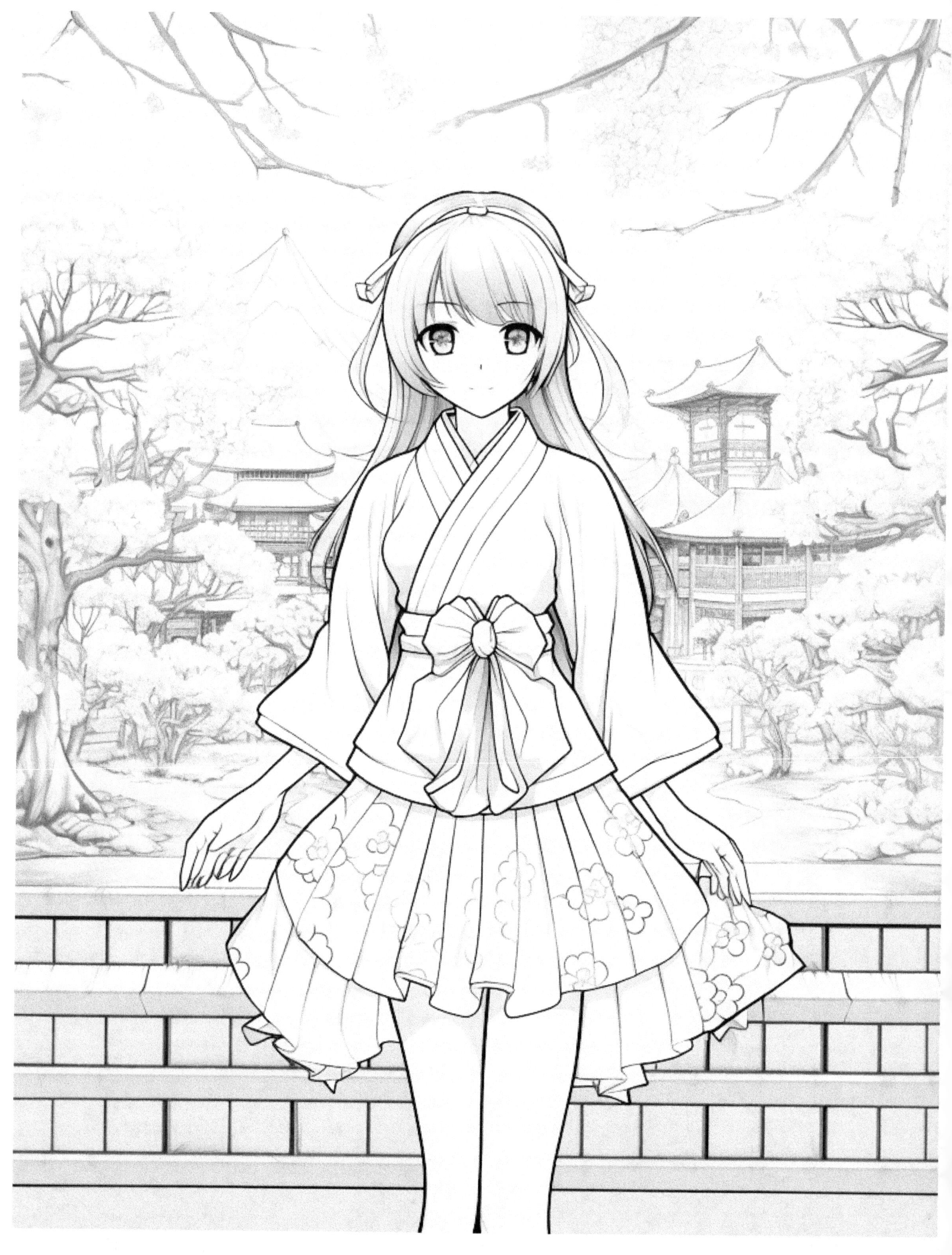

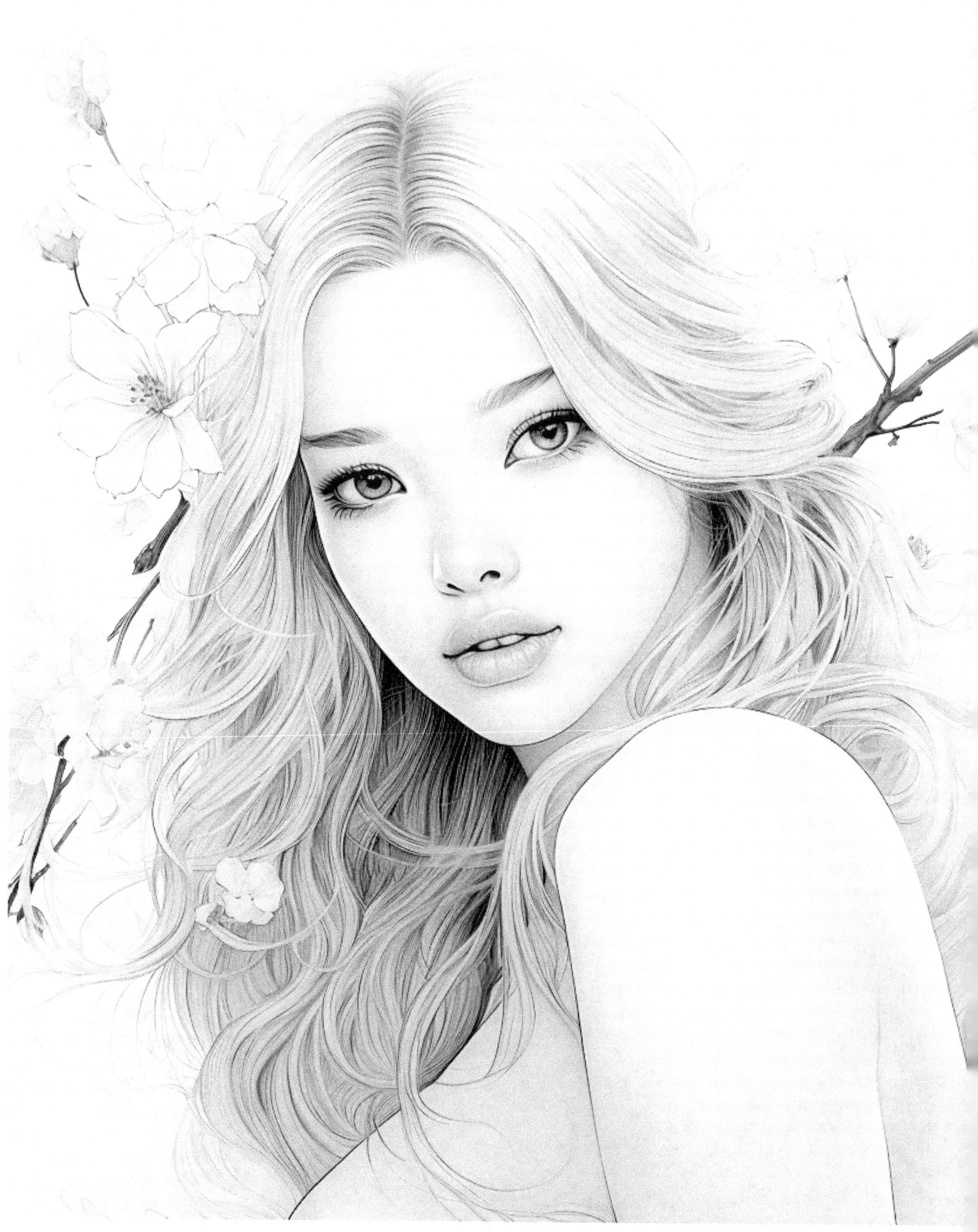

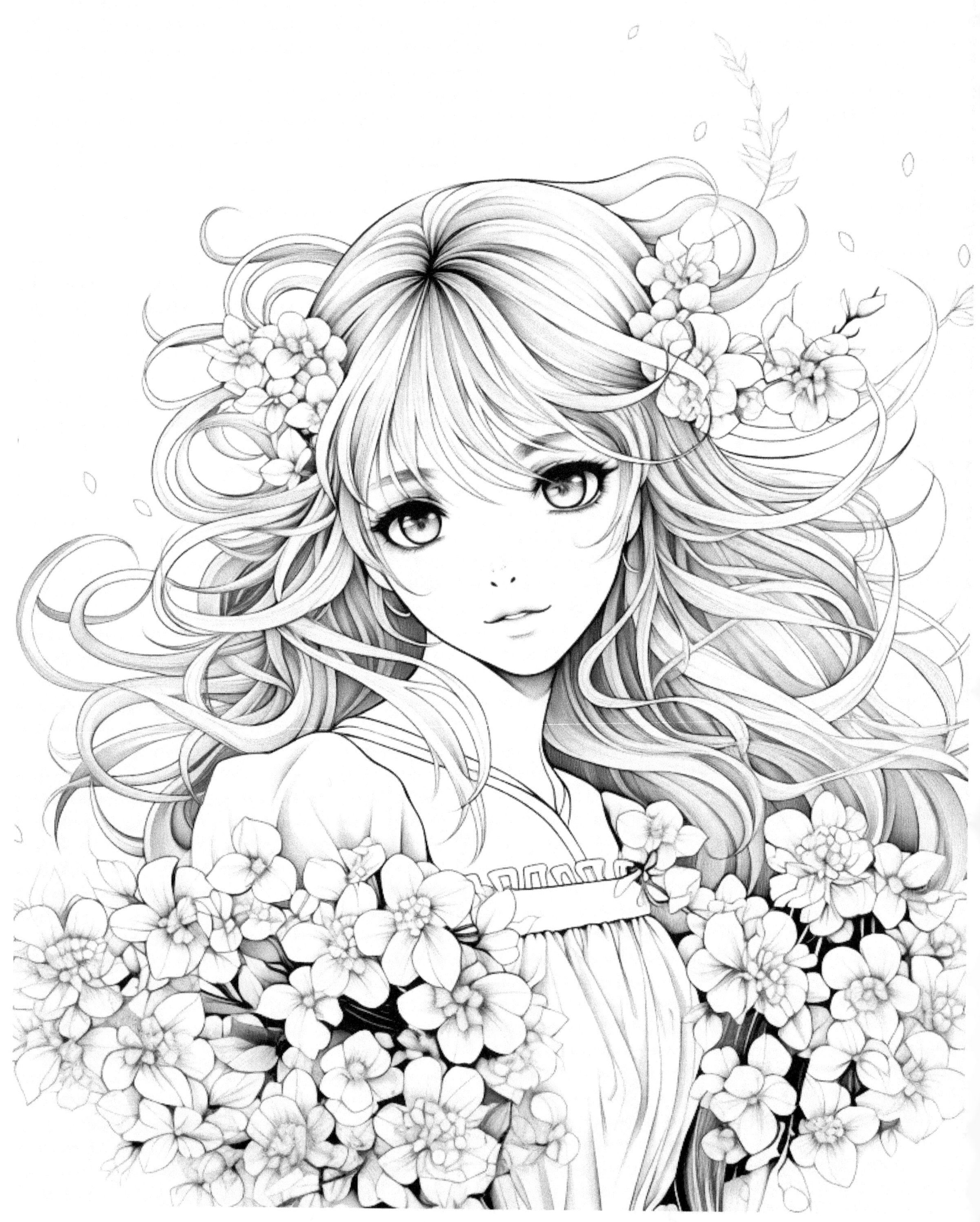

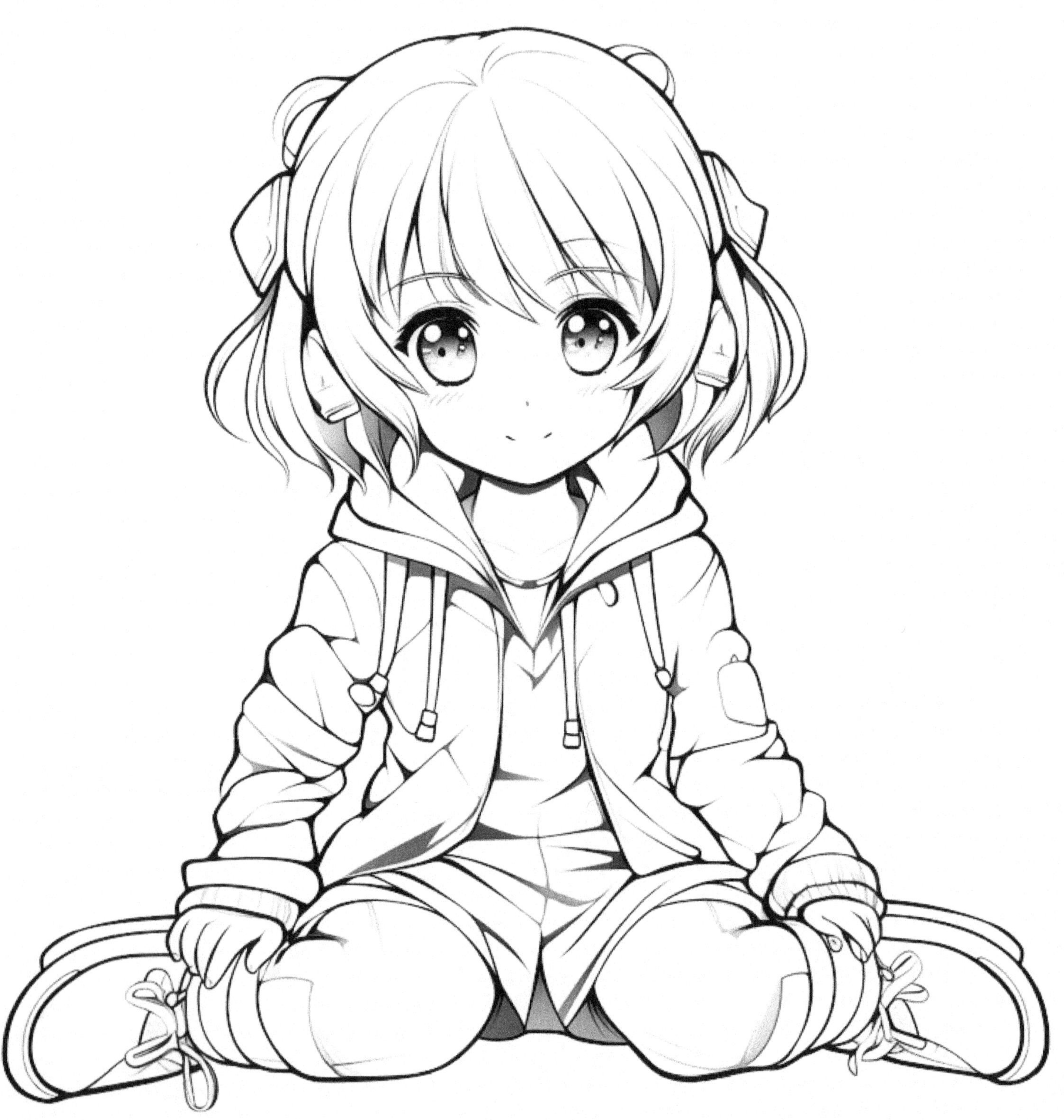

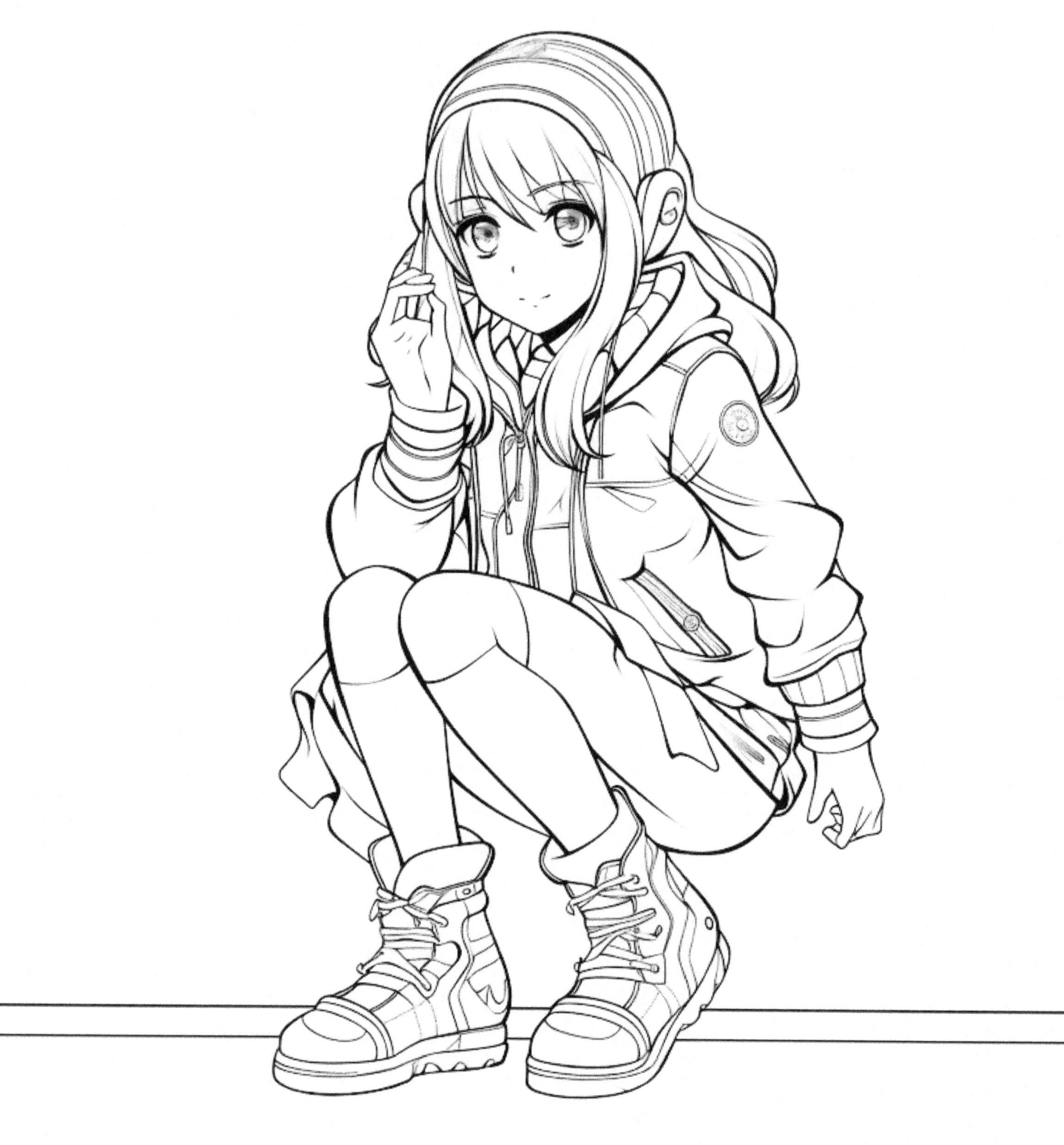

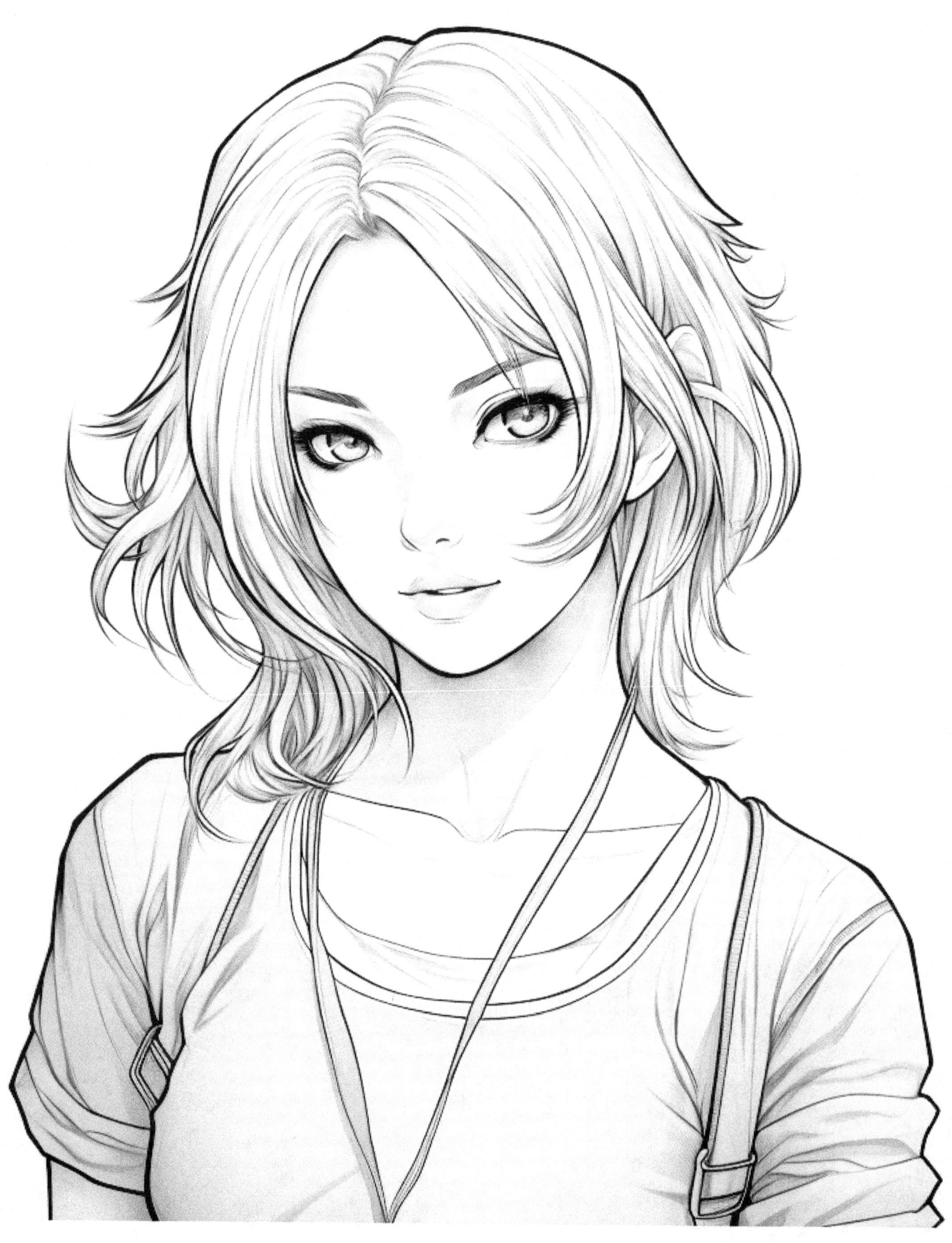

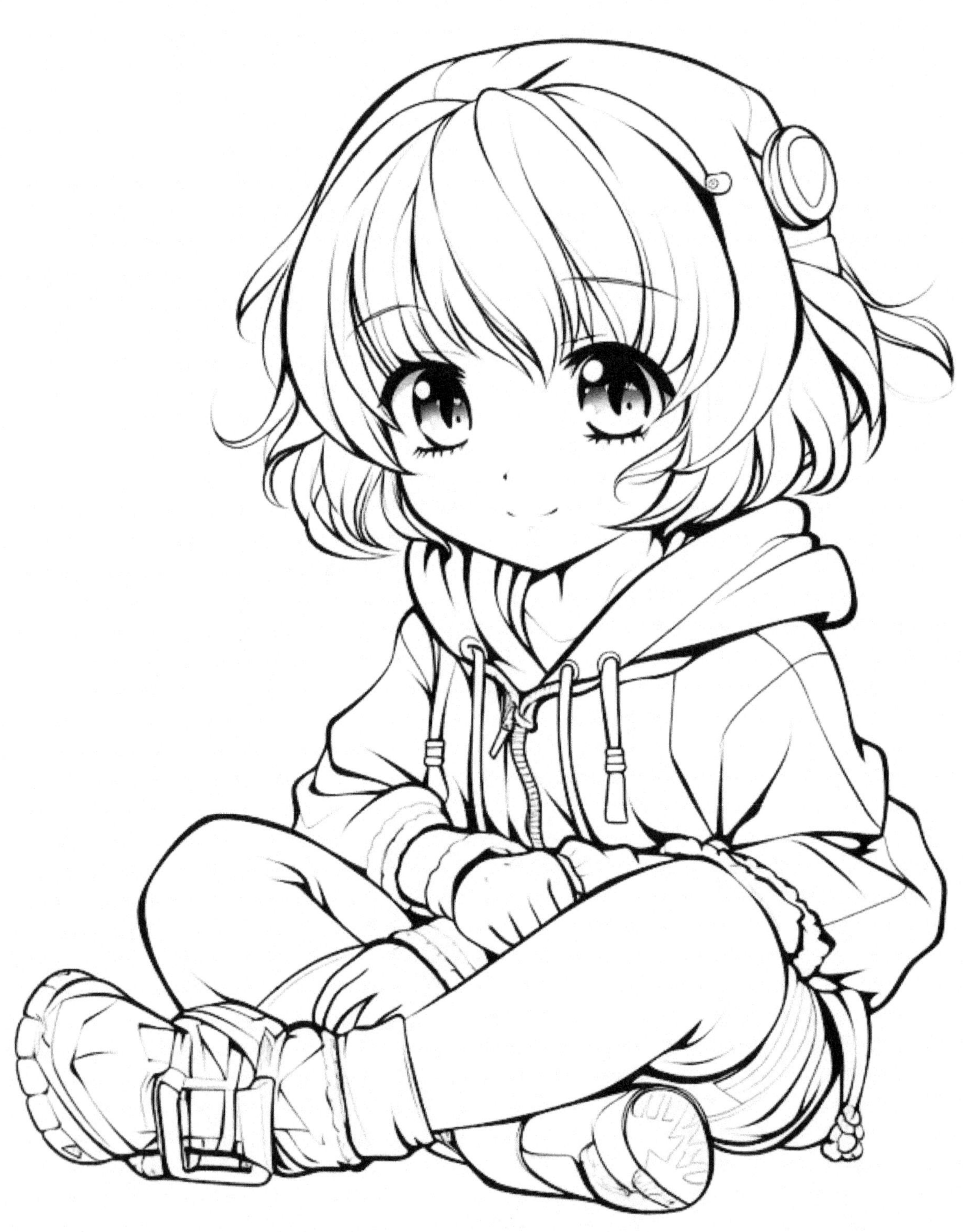

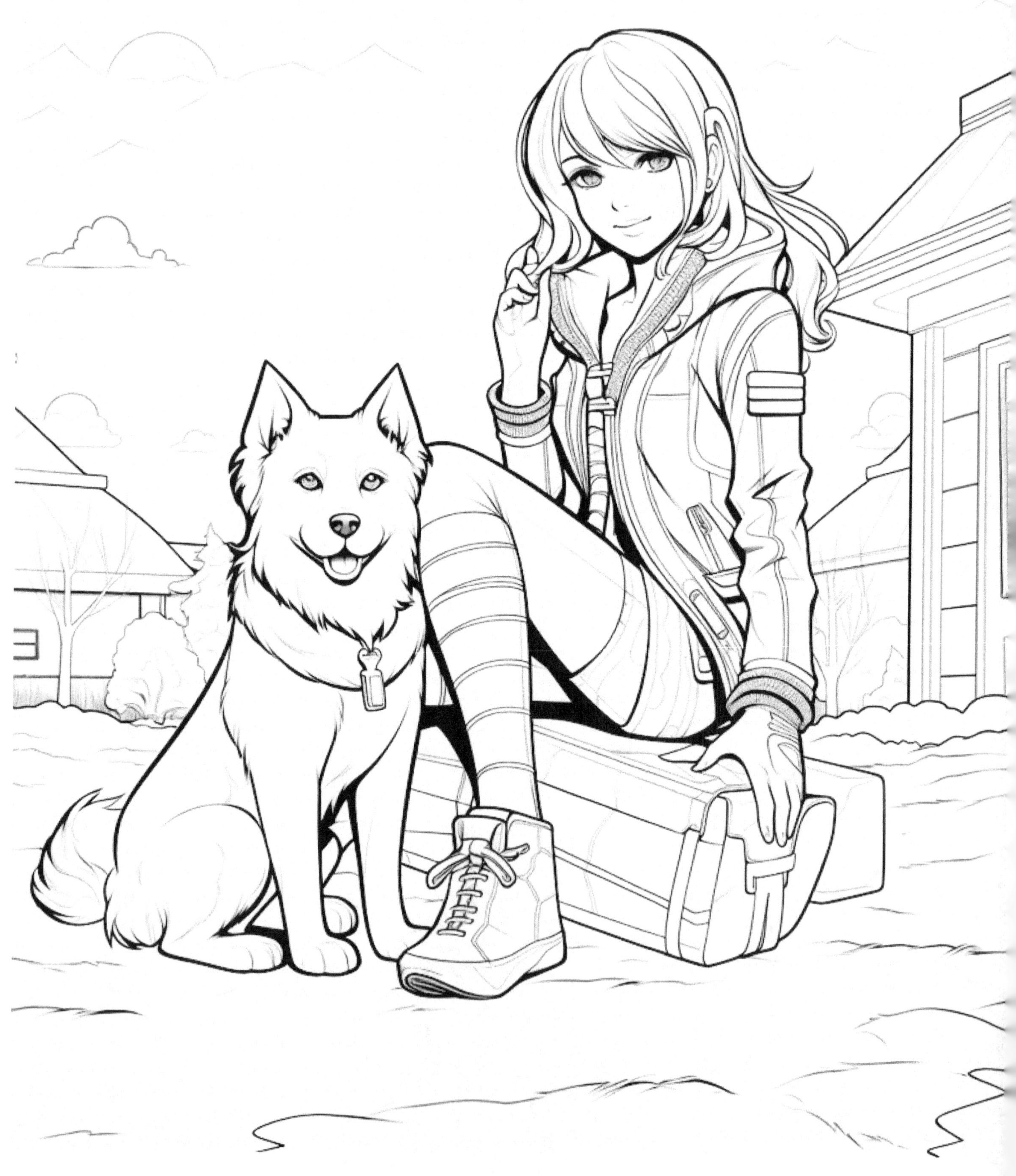

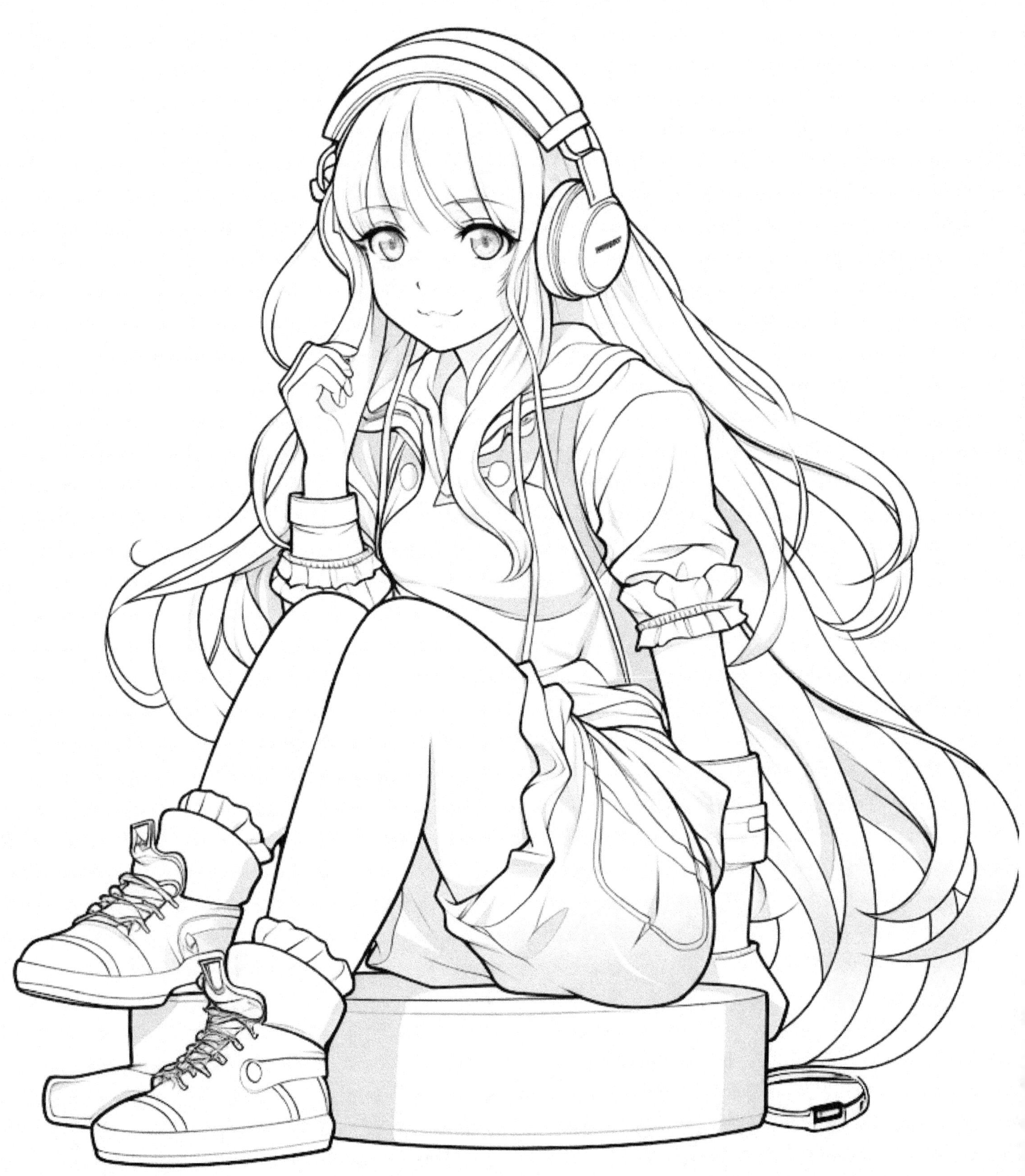

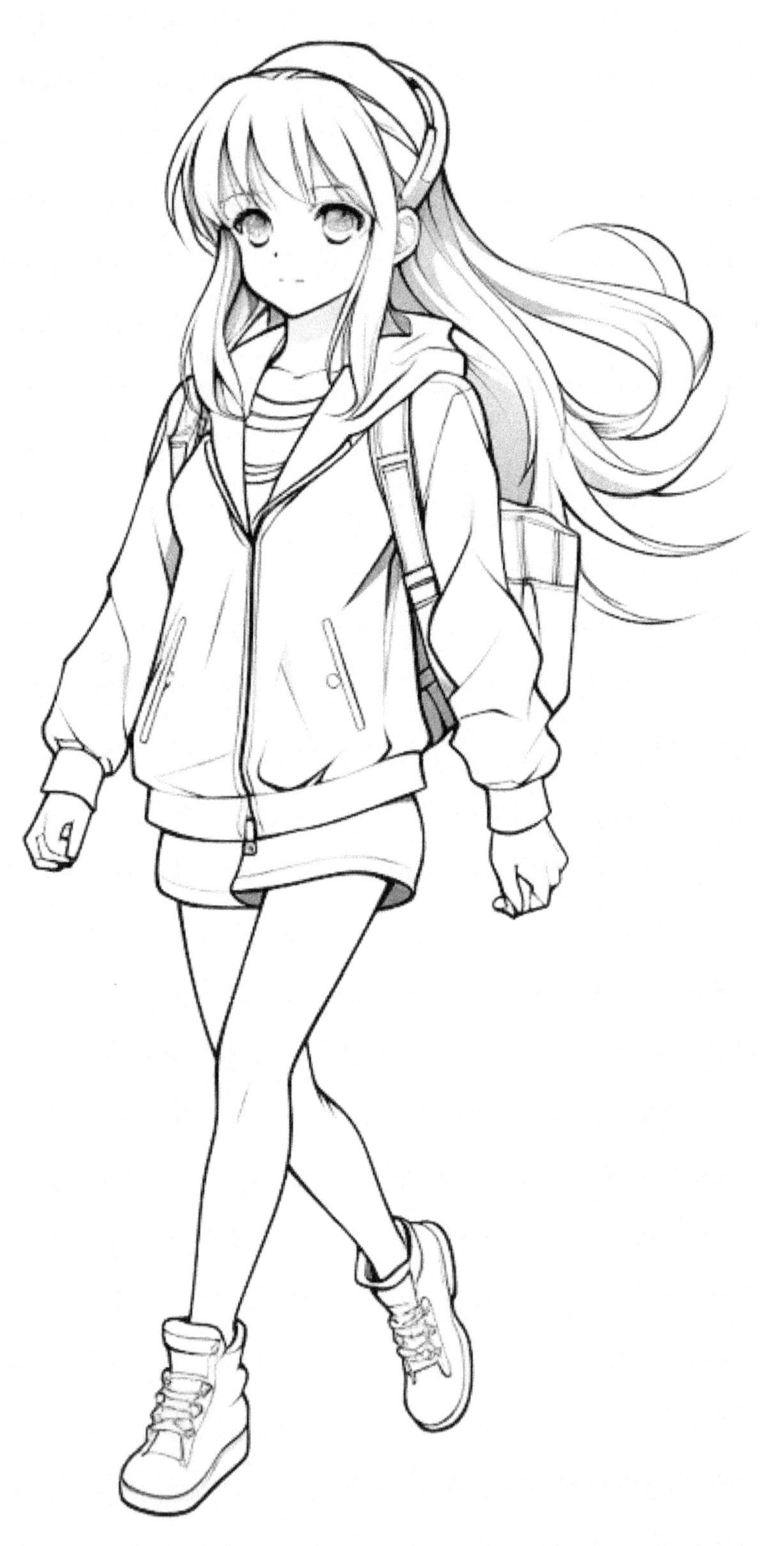

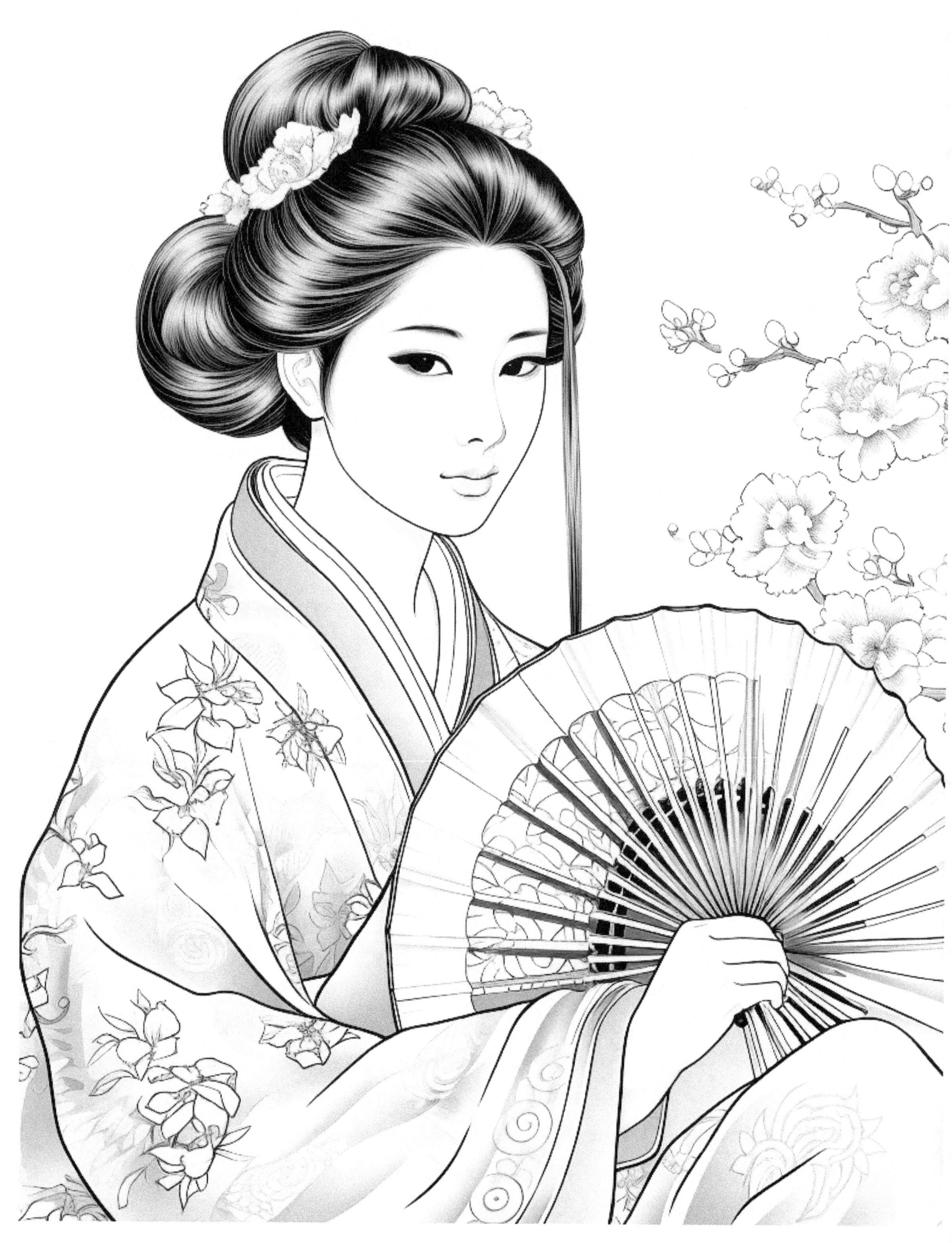

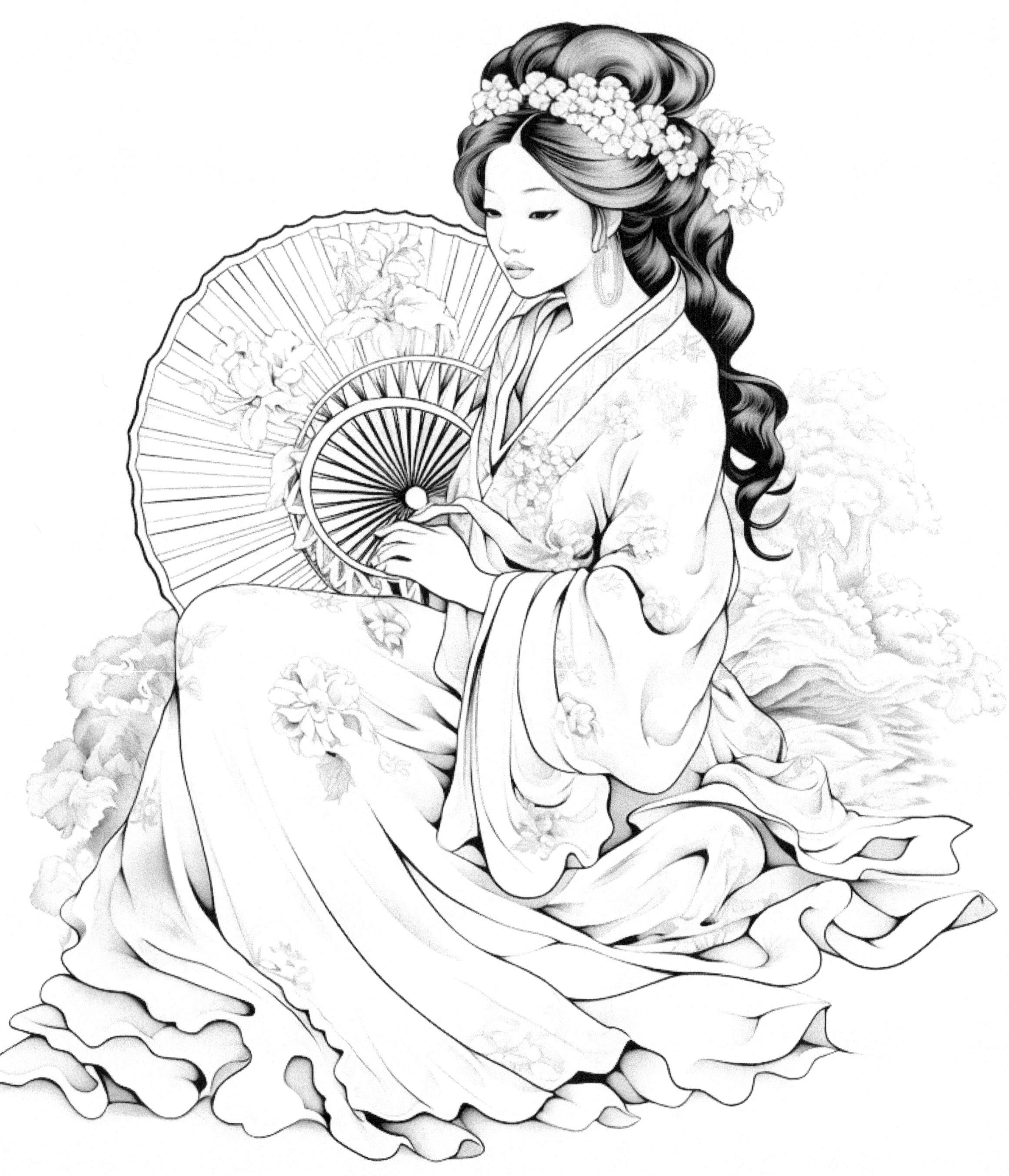

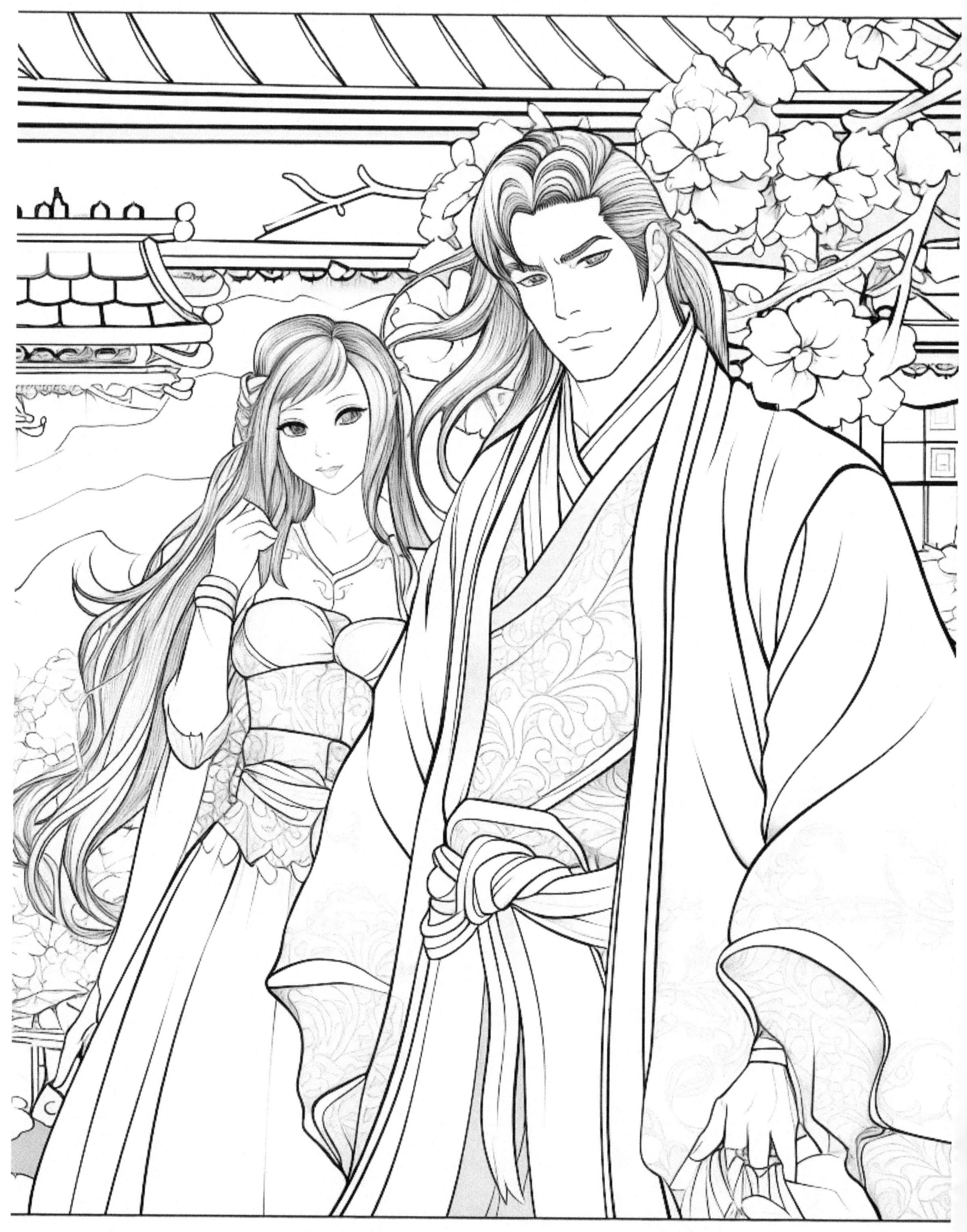

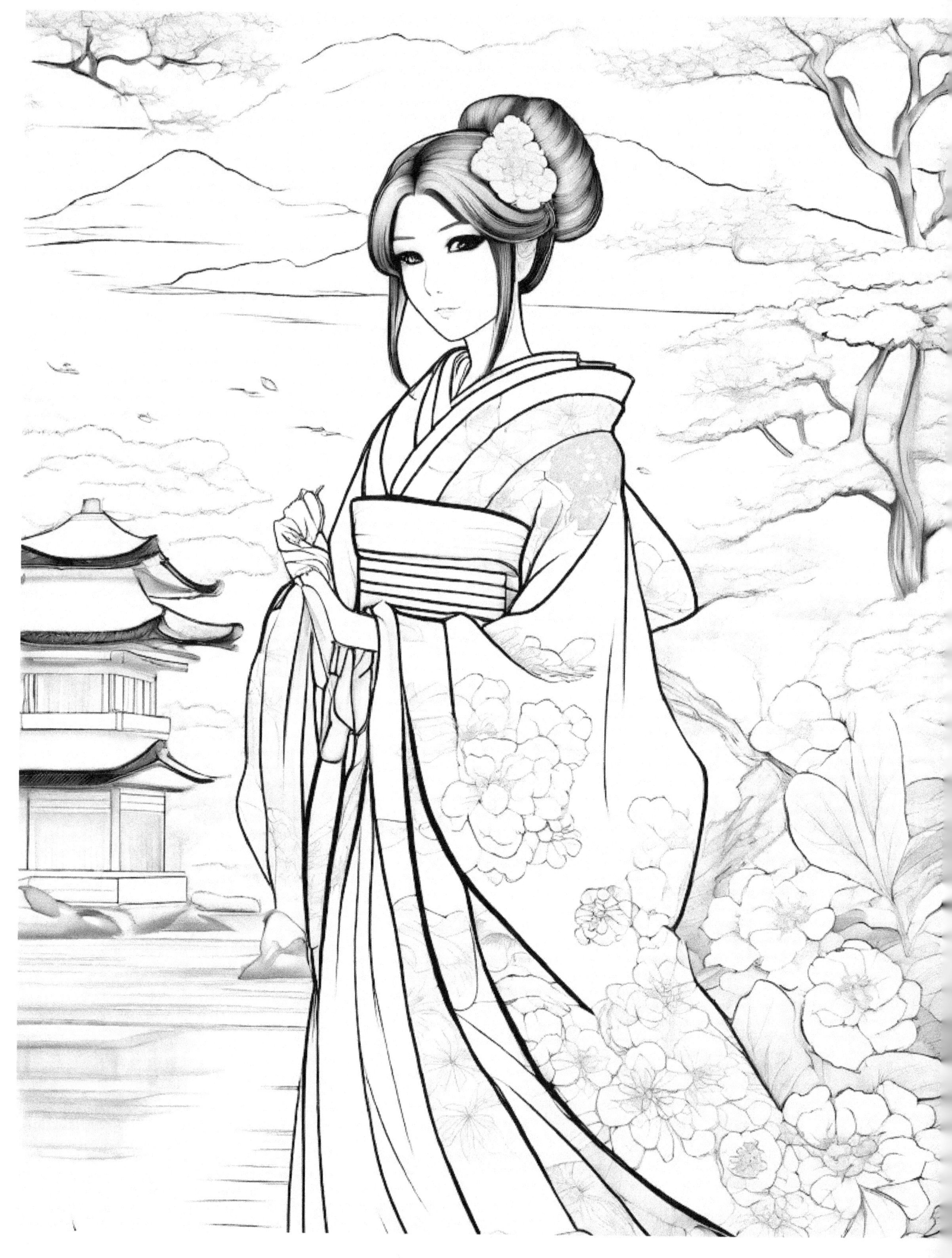

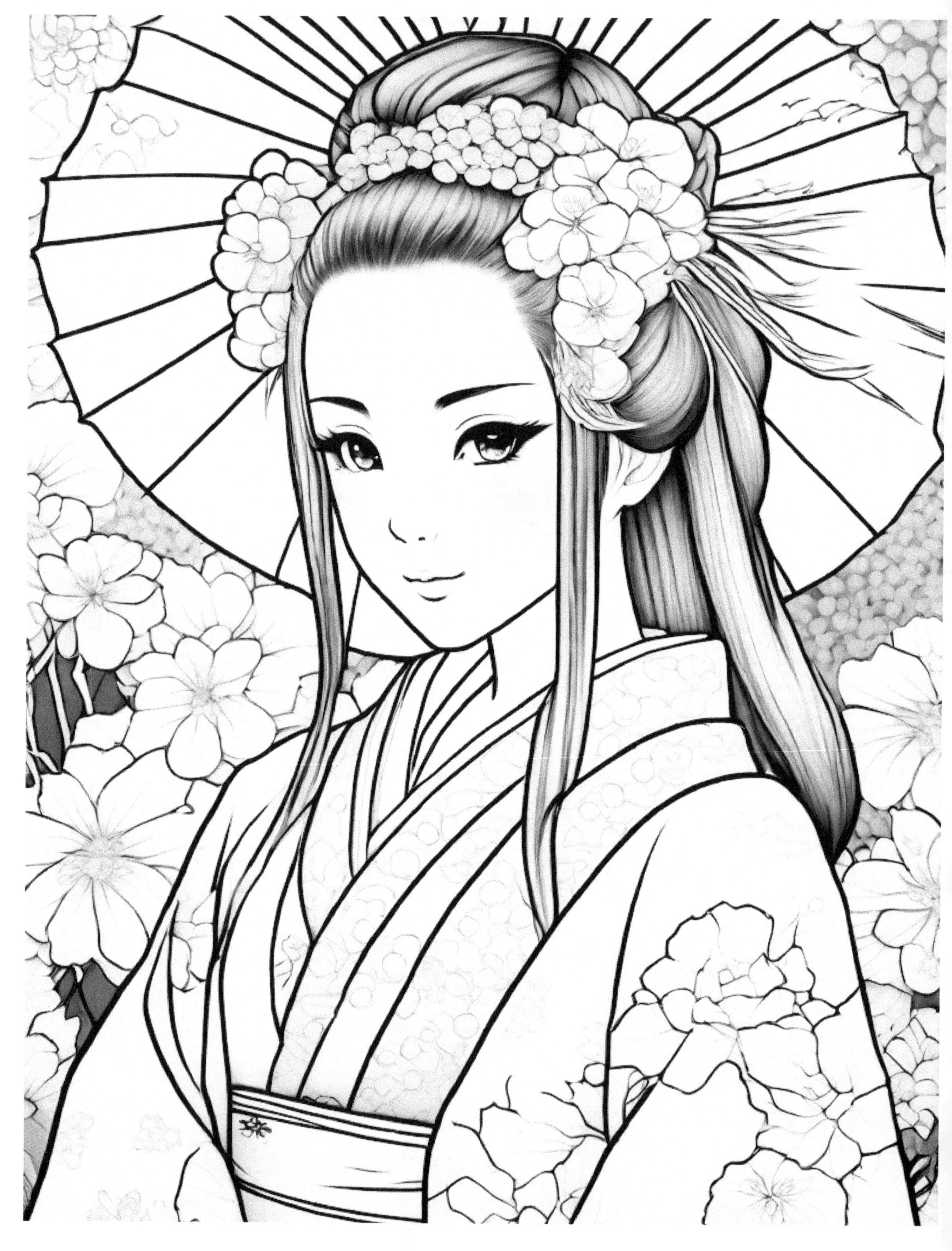